HEARKEN YE
& GIVE
EAR TO HIM

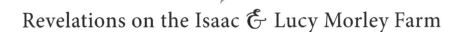

Revelations on the Isaac & Lucy Morley Farm

Other Books by
Damon L. Bahr &
Thomas P. Aardema

The Voice of the Lord Is unto All Men:
A Remarkable Year of Revelations in the Johnson Home

Search, Ponder Pray:
Historic Kirtland Church History Travel Guide

HEARKEN YE
& GIVE
EAR TO HIM

Revelations on the Isaac & Lucy Morley Farm

DAMON L.BAHR &
THOMAS P. AARDEMA

CFI

An imprint of Cedar Fort, Inc.

Springville, Utah

Paperback ISBN 13: 978–1-4621–4804–2
eBook ISBN 13: 978–1-4621–4805–9

Published by CFI, an imprint of Cedar Fort, Inc.
2373 W. 700 S., Suite 100, Springville, UT 84663
Distributed by Cedar Fort, Inc., www.cedarfort.com

Library of Congress Cataloging Number: 2024936341

Cover design by Shawda Craig
Cover design © 2024 Cedar Fort, Inc.
Edited by Liz Kazandzhy

Printed in the United States of America

10 9 8 7 6 5 4 3 2 1

Printed on acid-free paper

CONTENTS

Acknowledgments. 1

Preface 2

1   The Fulness of the Gospel Comes to Kirtland 4

2   The Isaac and Lucy Morley Family History. 9

3   "Thy Husband Shall Support Thee in the Church": The Residences
    of Joseph and Emma Smith. 17

4   "Every Man Shall Be a Steward": Unfolding the Law of Consecration
    and Stewardship 26

5   "Seek Ye Earnestly the Best Gifts": Dealing with False Gifts and
    Doctrines 42

6   "Obey the Law Which I Shall Give unto You": Additional Elements
    of "The Law" and Principles of Church Discipline. 55

7   Addressing "False Reports, Lies, and Foolish Stories": The Second
    Coming of Jesus Christ. 60

8   "True and Faithful": Personal Revelations to John Whitmer . . 67

9   "I Will Pour Out My Spirit upon Them in the Day That They
    Assemble Themselves Together": June Conference 69

10 "This Is the Land of Promise and the Place for the City of Zion":
    Zion in Missouri 76

11 "The Day Cometh That All Things Shall Be Subject unto Me":
    More Guidance for Zion from the Morleys' Farm 94

12 "Go and Preach My Gospel Which Ye Have Received": Leman
    Copley and the Mission to the Shakers 100

13 "A Babe on His Mother's Lap": A Miraculous Prophecy and the
    Gospel of Abraham 107

Notes 111

About the Authors 127

Acknowledgments

So many people deserve thanks when it comes to producing a book. The Cedar Fort folks are so great to work with, and I have a great coauthor, Tommy Aardema. This is our third book together and we aren't done yet! Most of all, many thanks to my wife, Kim, and our children who have always been so supportive. Our friends in the Kirtland area have meant so much to us over the years, so writing this book honors our shared heritage.

—Damon Bahr

I am grateful for my wife, Emilee, and our sons, Benson, Porter, Tanner, Carson, and Hunter. I am grateful for their willingness to make Ohio our home. I am grateful for Damon Bahr and his knowledge, faith, talent, and passion for all things Kirtland. It's inspiring to write with him. I am grateful for everyone who has helped me fall in love with Church history and instilled in me a passion to share these sacred sites with everyone. This book is dedicated to them.

—Thomas Aardema

PREFACE

This book is part of a series detailing the revelations received in Kirtland (and during the "Kirtland Era" of Church history) and the historical contexts in which they were received. It centers on the revelations the Prophet Joseph Smith received while residing on the farm of Isaac and Lucy Morley. The second book, *The Voice of the Lord Is unto All Men*, considers the revelations received by the Prophet in the John and Alice Johnson home.

The Doctrine and Covenants is unique in that, unlike the other standard works, it has no historical narrative. The other three books of scripture embed doctrinal discussions in historical and geographical contexts, but the Doctrine and Covenants details the revelations received by the Prophet Joseph Smith with little context. (That's why its divisions are called "sections," not chapters.) However, there is a myriad of records detailing the historical context, which provide an incredible view of the early days of the Restoration and places the reader in a position to receive an enhanced scripture-reading experience. Through putting these revelations in context in this book, our goal is to help readers deepen their love and appreciation for the Restoration of the Lord's Church and gospel.

The Prophet and his wife, Emma, only lived on the Morley farm for six months, but in that time, at least thirteen Doctrine and Covenants sections were revealed, numerous other manifestations were experienced, and the door was opened to other revelations received in Kirtland that constitute nearly half of that amazing book of scripture. Despite that, of all the Kirtland sites, the Morley farm is the one least visited and perhaps least appreciated. Our hope is that after reading this book, you will sense the powerful spirit that still pervades that most sacred place.

To preserve the chronological structure that characterizes our book series, it is also necessary to include in this volume a treatment of the four revelations, sections 41–44,[1] that the Prophet received while he and Emma resided in their first residence in Kirtland—the Newel K. and Elizabeth Ann Whitney home. Joseph and Emma arrived in Kirtland around February 4, 1831. They were first welcomed by the Whitneys and graciously invited to stay in their home, which they did for a month or so before moving to the Morleys' home, where "a house [was to be] built [for them] in which to live and translate" (Doctrine and Covenants 41:7).

Chapter 1

The Fulness of the Gospel Comes to Kirtland

Chronological Summary

- 1630—Charles II dedicates northeast Ohio to the colony of Connecticut
- 1796—The Connecticut Land Company buys 1.2 million acres
- 1798—Moses Cleveland leads an initial survey of acreage
- 1799—Turhand Kirtland is given a portion of acreage, which becomes Kirtland Township
- Early 1800s—The Morleys and Whitneys are among the early Kirtland settlers
- 1826—Sidney Rigdon is the pastor of the Reformed Baptist congregation in Mentor, Ohio
- September 1830—Parley P. Pratt travels to New York and is baptized
- October 1830—Parley P. Pratt, Oliver Cowdery, Ziba Peterson, and Peter Whitmer Jr. embark on a mission to the Lamanites (Doctrine and Covenants 28, 30, 32)

- November 1830—The first missionaries in the Kirtland area convert 127 people, including Sidney Rigdon
- December 1830—Sidney Rigdon and Edward Partridge travel to New York (Doctrine and Covenants 35–36)
- January 1831—The Lord commands to Saints to go "to the Ohio" (Doctrine and Covenants 37–39), and John Whitmer is the first to move to Kirtland
- February 1831—Joseph and Emma Smith arrive in Kirtland
- March 1831—Joseph and Emma move to the Morley farm
- September 12, 1831—Joseph and Emma move to the Johnson farm

The Land of Kirtland

Long before the Prophet Joseph Smith received the revelation in Doctrine and Covenants 37 calling for the Saints to gather "to the Ohio" (verse 1), King Charles II of England in 1630 deeded four million acres to the colony of Connecticut—land that would eventually become Ohio. The state of Connecticut acquired substantial debt during the American Revolution, but following the war, they exchanged acreage for federal assumption of that debt, and the remaining 3,366 acres became known as the "Western Reserve." In 1796 a portion of the reserve was sold to a group of private speculators known as the Connecticut Land Company, and in 1798, a man named Moses Cleveland led an initial surveying expedition that was sponsored by the company. One of his associates, Turhand Kirtland, surveyed an area east of what became Cleveland, and he received a portion of the land as payment for his work. He sold parcels the following year to settlers in the area that would become known as Kirtland Township.

Conversions of Sidney Rigdon and Parley P. Pratt

The Prophet described "an unusual excitement on the subject of religion" (Joseph Smith—History 1:5) in the early 1800s that swept through northern Ohio along with western New York and northern Pennsylvania. Sidney Rigdon, a Reformed Baptist preacher, perpetuated this excitement as he preached restorationist Christianity among several of his congregations in settlements around Kirtland. Sidney's proselytes included Parley P. and Thankful Pratt, Newel K. and Elizabeth Ann Whitney, and Isaac and Lucy Morley.

Parley P. Pratt felt impressed to sell his home in Amherst, Ohio, in the summer of 1830 and travel with his wife, Thankful, to New York on a self-appointed preaching mission. While traveling on the Erie canal, Parley felt prompted to leave the canal boat at Newark, New York, ten miles east of Palmyra, leaving Thankful to travel on to their final destination alone. Shortly thereafter, he was introduced to the Book of Mormon by a Baptist deacon named Hamblin, and he was instantly enthralled by it. He later wrote, "I read all day; eating was a burden, I had no desire for food; sleep was a burden when the night came, for I preferred reading to sleep. . . . I knew and comprehended that the book was true. . . . My joy was now full."[2] Parley then traveled to Palmyra, New York, where he was taught by the Prophet's brother Hyrum and baptized by Oliver Cowdery on September 1, 1830. Ultimately, Parley's conversion led to the conversion of Sidney Rigdon and the subsequent gathering of the New York Saints to Kirtland.

Missionary Success in Kirtland

During the month of Parley's baptism, the Lord revealed to Joseph that Oliver Cowdery should "go unto the Lamanites" to "the borders by the Lamanites" (Doctrine and Covenants 28:8–9), the area where the western border of the new state of Missouri met the unincorporated Indian territory that later became the state of Kansas. (The Lord also revealed the general location of the city of Zion.) Three other brethren were called to serve as Oliver's companions in sections 30 and 32— Peter Whitmer Jr., Ziba Peterson, and Parley P. Pratt. The Lord promised, "I myself will go with them" (Doctrine and Covenants 32:3), and the four missionary companions left New York in early October.

While traveling through northern Ohio near the end of October, Parley suggested they visit his former religious mentor, Sidney Rigdon. Although Sidney was "very much prejudiced" at the suggestion that another book of scripture, the Book of Mormon, should be accepted along with the Bible, he generously gave the missionaries permission to present their message to his congregants in Mentor, a town just north of Kirtland. Probably feeling the Spirit, he told the congregation that the missionaries' message "was of an extraordinary character, and certainly demanded their most serious consideration." Sidney himself said, "I will read your book, and see what claims it has upon my faith," assuring them he would "give it a full investigation."[3] Sidney soon received his own confirming vision: he was shown the corruption of the common religious teachings of his time, then, in contrast, he saw the Book of Mormon, as "pure as an angel."[4]

After a short time, Parley related, "The people thronged us night and day, insomuch that we had no time for rest and retirement. . . . Thousands flocked about us daily; some to be taught, some for curiosity, some to obey the gospel, and some to dispute or resist it."[5] During the three weeks the missionaries were in the area, 127 people were baptized, eventually including Sidney Rigdon and about 100 members of his Mentor congregation.[6] Missionary work also continued as the new converts preached the gospel in northern Ohio, some without formal mission calls. By February 2, a total of about 400 people had joined the Church.

Sidney and an interested investigator and friend, Edward Partridge, traveled to New York in December 1830, desiring to meet Joseph Smith. Edward was baptized the day after, and Joseph received two revelations, one for Sidney and one for Edward. Addressing Sidney, the Lord honored his pre-baptismal preaching. "Behold thou wast sent forth, even as John, to prepare the way before me, and before Elijah which should come, and thou knewest it not" (Doctrine and Covenants 35:4). Many of the early Ohio converts had been followers of Sidney Rigdon who had taught them "restoration doctrine," thus preparing the way for the Lamanite missionaries' success.

Gathering

Concerned with the constant and vicious persecution he and the Saints were facing in New York and northern Pennsylvania, and hearing of the missionaries' success in Ohio, Joseph petitioned the Lord in prayer in December 1830 and received a revelation that the Saints "should assemble together at the Ohio" (Doctrine and Covenants 37:3). He received two additional revelations in early January wherein the Lord reiterated His command to "go to the Ohio" (Doctrine and Covenants 38:32), promising that "inasmuch as my people shall assemble themselves at the Ohio, I have kept in store a blessing such as is not known among the children of men" (Doctrine and Covenants 39:15).

John Whitmer was the first to move, and Joseph left for Kirtland by sleigh soon thereafter with his wife, Emma, who was pregnant with twins. They arrived sometime in early February, traveling with Sidney Rigdon, Edward Partridge, Ezra Thayre, Joseph Knight Sr., and a wagon full of copies of the Book of Mormon. They were joined by most of the New York Saints who began preparations to move to Ohio in response to the command to gather.

Joseph's first stop in Kirtland was Newel K. Whitney's store, where Joseph entered and greeted him, saying, "Newel K. Whitney, thou art the man,"[7] to which Newel replied, "I could not call you by name as you have me." Joseph answered, "I am Joseph the Prophet; you have prayed me here, now what do you want of me?"[8] Joseph had seen in vision Newel on his knees praying for the Prophet to come.

In September 1831 the Lord revealed that He would "retain a strong hold in the land of Kirtland, for the space of five years" (Doctrine and Covenants 64:21). During that five-year period, nearly half of the current Doctrine and Covenants was revealed, and most of the Joseph Smith Translation of the Bible was completed. Most of the priesthood offices and quorums were formalized and filled; missionaries were sent into the eastern United States, Canada, and England, bringing thousands into the kingdom; and a temple was built wherein priesthood keys were restored and the initiatory portion of the endowment was administered. Evidence suggests there may have been as many as sixty-one Church branches in the area surrounding Kirtland by the time the Saints left.[9]

Chapter 2

The Isaac and Lucy Morley Family History

Isaac and Lucy Morley Family

Isaac Morley was born in Montague, Massachusetts, on March 11, 1786, one of nine children of Thomas E. Morley and Editha Marsh.[10] His wife, Lucy Gunn, was also born in Montague that same year on January 24, one of seven children of Asahel Gunn and Lucy Root.[11] Isaac and Lucy were some of the earliest settlers in the Kirtland area, undoubtedly influenced to settle there by Isaac's uncle Ezekiel. Ezekiel was among those employed with Turhand Kirtland in 1797 to survey the part of the "Western Reserve" where Kirtland was eventually located. In 1811 Isaac acquired one hundred acres from Ezekiel on the "Kirtland Flats," a heavily wooded area that became the site of several industrial and merchandising enterprises and that was east of what became known as "Temple Hill." Isaac built a small cabin before returning home to Salem that fall to marry his childhood sweetheart, Lucy. They were married June 20, 1812, and left for Ohio three days later. She eventually gave birth to at least nine children, seven of whom survived to adulthood—Philena, Lucy Diantha, Aditha Ann, Calista, Cordelia, Theressa, and Isaac Jr.[12]

Later in 1812 Isaac left Lucy alone while he went off to serve in the War of 1812. Morley family records suggest that Isaac's absence was a great trial to Lucy—fears about living alone in a wilderness without close neighbors, with howling wolves and the presence of Indians, apparently caused her to remain in her cabin with the door barred and blankets covering the windows the entire time Isaac was away. Fortunately for her, he only served three to six months when chills and fever ended his military service and he returned home.

After Isaac's return, he and Lucy worked together to create a farm where they grew fruit trees, field crops, and flax for food, cash, and linen cloth. Wool from their sheep provided Lucy material for sewing clothes for her family. Isaac worked as a cooper to make barrels to sell and use in storing the maple sugar and honey he extracted from the trees and hives on their property. In 1814 they built a small log cabin schoolhouse on a hilltop on the north side of their property, which was used to educate the Morleys' children and the children of friends and neighbors. They were also able to build and move into a frame house shortly thereafter. Isaac's parents moved to Kirtland in 1815 and established a maple sugar endeavor across the road south of Isaac and Lucy's. They were also joined by several of Isaac's siblings.

Isaac took an active part in the political and religious activities of Kirtland. He was one of the qualified electors of Kirtland Township and was elected one of the trustees of the first town board. While the Morleys were becoming established economically, they had some connection to the Presbyterian Church. Family records suggest that Thomas Morley and his family were originally Congregationalists. In early 1828 they fulfilled a desire to participate fully in following the New Testament pattern of gospel living by joining Sidney Rigdon and other early settlers in the Reformed Baptist movement. Possibly influenced by Robert Owen's promotion of communal living,[13] or other nearby communal groups like the Shakers, Isaac was especially interested in the lifestyle of the Saints portrayed in the book of Acts to have "all things common." Following Sidney's direction in 1830, Isaac, his brother-in-law Titus Billings,[14] and Lyman Wight[15] influenced between fifty and a hundred people to join with them in a communal group called "The Family," or "The Big Family." Most of these built a string of cabins on the Morley farm, although a few members gathered in Thompson, Ohio.

In the meantime, the Lord was guiding and empowering the Prophet Joseph Smith and others to move forward and proclaim the Restoration. When the four missionaries arrived in the Kirtland area on October 29, they separated into two groups. Peter Whitmer Jr. and Ziba Peterson stopped in Euclid, west of Kirtland, to hold a meeting, where Isaac first heard the restored gospel and five attendees were baptized.

Following their first attempts to preach to Sidney and his congregation in nearby Mentor, Oliver and Parley were joined by Ziba, and the three missionaries traveled south to the home of Abigail Daniels, a mile north of the Morleys. Fifteen-year-old Lucy Diantha Morley worked for Abigail performing various household duties, including assisting Abigail in producing cloth, some of which would go to the Morleys in exchange for Lucy's services. Abigail refused to listen to the missionaries' message or provide food for them. Despite Abigail's vehement protestations to the contrary, however, Lucy expressed interest and said that if they went to her home, her father would care for them and listen to their message.

When the missionaries arrived on the Morley farm later that same day, they first met Lyman Wight, who was busily filling a wagon with goods he planned to take to nearby Mayfield in an effort to establish a branch of the "Family" there. Despite Lyman's initial reluctance to forestall his preparations to leave for Mayfield, the missionaries persisted and, as Lyman recorded, "curiosity got uppermost and I concluded to stop for a while."[16] Lyman didn't pull himself away from the missionaries until later in the afternoon, at which time a relatively large group had joined in the discussion, which centered on the Book of Mormon, the restoration of the priesthood, and the doctrine of Christ (see 2 Nephi 31). No doubt influenced by his prior experience in Euclid, Isaac was among the first of the group to become convinced of the truth he was hearing.

After the group dispersed, Isaac spoke with his father, Thomas, well into the night about the message. Thomas had not joined with the "Family" and was very much opposed to the missionaries' message. As young Lucy later recounted, her grandfather was "full of his old tradi-tion he thought that there need be no more revelation and would not hear what Father had to say but turned a deaf ear to all that my Father could say to him and told him to leave his house and never darken his door again and never did."[17] Peter Whitmer Jr. soon joined the other three missionaries, and the Morleys allowed them to make the farm their home during their three-week stay in Kirtland.

Isaac, Lucy, and four of their children were baptized in November 1830. They were among the first Latter-day Saint converts and were joined by all of the adult members of the "Family." Members of the Russell family—who became Morley relatives through Thomas Morley Jr., Isaac's brother—also converted. Some of the earliest Church meet-ings in Kirtland were held in the Morley schoolhouse.

Isaac's interaction with twelve-year-old Mary Elizabeth Rollins (lat-er Lightner) is a classic story of the power of the Book of Mormon in the rich missionary harvest that occurred in early Kirtland. Mary and her mother were baptized in the end of October, shortly after the four Lamanite missionaries arrived in Ohio. The same evening as their bap-tism, Mary recorded that she went to the Morleys, having heard they possessed one of the few copies of the Book of Mormon in Kirtland. When she asked to hold it, she was overwhelmed with a desire to read it. Isaac was hesitant, not having read much of it himself, but Mary's pleadings eventually led him to say, "Child, if you will bring this book home before breakfast tomorrow morning, you may take it."[18]

Mary's hopes were abundantly fulfilled as she and her family read the Book of Mormon together and when she continued studying it on her own. "If any person in this world was ever perfectly happy in the possession of any coveted treasure I was when I had permission to read that wonderful book. . . . I was severely reprimanded for being so pre-sumptuous as to ask such a favor, when Brother Morley had not read it himself. We all took turns reading it until very late in the night as soon as it was light enough to see, I was up and learned the first verse in the book."[19]

Following her morning reading, Mary returned it to Isaac and surprised him with the depth of her study. He said, "I don't believe you can tell me one word of it." Mary recited the first verse and also described "the outlines of the history of Nephi," to which Isaac responded, "Child, take this book home and finish it, I can wait."[20]

After finishing her reading of the Book of Mormon in three months—quite a feat for a twelve-year-old—she was privileged to meet with the Prophet, who had recently arrived in Kirtland with his wife, Emma. Her earnest reading was well rewarded when Newel K. Whitney brought Joseph to Mary's home. When he saw the Book of Mormon on a shelf, he asked how they came to have it. When Mary's uncle Algernon Sidney Gilbert explained the circumstances, he sent for Mary, but she wasn't home at the time. Mary later described first seeing the Prophet upon her return: "When he saw me he looked at me so earnestly, I felt almost afraid. After a moment or two he came and put his hands on my head and gave me a great blessing, the first I ever received, and made me a present of the book, and said he would give Brother Morley another."[21]

Before the missionaries left for western Missouri, Sidney Rigdon was appointed as the leader of the Kirtland Branch, one of the four branches of the Church established in northeast Ohio. Isaac replaced him the following month when Sidney and Edward Partridge, who lived in Painesville, traveled to New York to meet the Prophet (see Doctrine and Covenants 35–36). After three months, the *Geauga Gazette* reported that there were 200 converts in the village of Kirtland and at least 400 converts in the larger area.[22]

Following their arrival in Kirtland on or about February 4, 1831, Joseph and Emma Smith housed temporarily in the home of Newel and Elizabeth Ann Whitney. There the Prophet received the revelations that now constitute Doctrine and Covenants 41–44, which include the earliest instructions for living the law of consecration and stewardship. It also directed that a house be built for Joseph and Emma, which was fulfilled on the Morley farm when they moved in with the Morleys in their frame home while waiting for the completion of their own. In this house, on April 30, Emma gave birth to twins who died shortly after birth. Also in this house, Emma and Joseph adopted the Murdock twins after their mother, Julia Clapp Murdock, passed away shortly after giving birth.

Exercising great faith in the spring of 1831, the Morleys generously offered their farm in consecration as a settling place for the nearly

200 Saints migrating from the three Church branches in New York—Palmyra (and Kingston), Fayette, and Colesville. Most of the New York Saints made the Morley farm their home. The Palmyra Branch arrived in June, and Mary Elizabeth Rollins related a remarkable experience that occurred the day of their arrival. She and her mother had walked to the Morleys' to hear more about the Book of Mormon from the Prophet. When the Prophet saw the relatively large group, Mary recorded that he said, "We might as well have a meeting." Following prayer and singing, Mary indicated, "Joseph began talking. Suddenly he stopped and seemed almost transfixed. He was looking ahead and his face outshone the candle which was on a shelf just behind him. I thought I could almost see the cheek bones. He looked as though a searchlight was inside his face."[23]

The Prophet looked at the group and asked, "Brothers and Sisters, do you know who has been in your midst this night?" Joseph did not respond to the answer provided by one Smith family member—"An angel of the Lord." Martin Harris was sitting next to the Prophet on a box, from which he slid to his knees, wrapped his arms around the Prophet's legs, and said, "I know, it was our Lord and Savior, Jesus Christ." Placing his hand on Martin's head, Joseph responded, "Martin, God has revealed that to you. Brothers and Sisters, the Savior has been in your midst. I want you to remember it. He cast a veil over your eyes for you could not endure to look upon him. You must be fed with milk and not meat. I want you to remember this as if it were the last thing that escaped my lips."[24]

Mary then described the effect of that experience and of what happened next. "These words are figured upon my brain and I never took my eye off his countenance. Then he knelt down and prayed. I have never heard anything like it before or since. I felt that he was talking to the Lord and that power rested down upon the congregation. Every soul felt it. The spirit rested upon us in every fiber of our bodies, and we received a sermon from the lips of the representative of God."[25]

The faithfulness of Isaac and Lucy reflects a pattern of consistent sacrifice, courage, and commitment. Isaac was ordained a high priest in June as part of the group to first receive that priesthood office. He was among the first group of missionaries called to western Missouri. He served as a counselor to Bishop Edward Partridge at Kirtland and

Independence, Missouri, where he also later served as bishop. After he and Lucy moved their family to Independence, they experienced the mob activity that erupted in 1833. He was one of the six brethren who offered their lives in exchange for relief of mob action against the Saints, who were jailed for three nights and informed they were to be executed following day.[26] Fortunately, they were blessed to escape.[27]

Continued mob action eventually forced all the Saints to leave Jackson County. Most, including the Morleys, fled north across the Missouri River to Clay County in November 1833. Isaac was appointed a member of the Missouri High Council the following month, then served a three-month mission to the eastern United States with Edward Partridge in 1835.

In 1836 the Saints were again forced to leave their homes in Clay County and fled northward to Caldwell County, a "reservation" of sorts specifically set aside for the Saints by the Missouri legislature at the instigation of Alexander Doniphan. There Isaac was ordained a patriarch in 1837. Mobocracy soon followed the Saints again, and Isaac was one of approximately fifty brethren along with the Prophet who were imprisoned in Jackson and Ray counties during the month of November. Due to continued persecution, the Saints fled Missouri to eastern Illinois in early 1839.

The Morleys settled near Nauvoo, where Isaac founded "Yelrome" ("Morley" spelled backwards) and served as bishop. He was later appointed as stake president at Lima, Illinois, then moved to Nauvoo in 1845 where he was admitted to the Council of Fifty, a pre-millennial leadership group established by the Prophet to fulfill a combined ecclesiastical and political role.

In 1844 Isaac was introduced to and practiced plural marriage in Nauvoo, where he took Leonora Snow (the older sister of Lorenzo and Eliza R. Snow) as his second wife and Hannah Blakesley as his third. Hannah and Isaac had three children. Isaac later married Hannah Knight Libby, Harriet Lucinda Cox, Hannah Sibley, and Nancy Anne Bache (also found as Back).

The Morleys left Nauvoo with many of the Saints in February 1846, and in early 1847 Lucy passed away while the Morleys were temporarily residing in Winter Quarters. After arriving in the Salt Lake Valley in 1848, Isaac was elected senator to the provisional state of Deseret in

March 1849. He was also called to scout out the Sanpete Valley later that year, and he later helped settle the city of Manti. While living in Sanpete County, he served as a patriarch. His time in Sanpete was interrupted by a three-year return to the Salt Lake Valley as assigned by Brigham Young. He then moved to Santaquin (originally known as "Summit") in Utah County and finally to Fairview, Sanpete County. During this time in Utah, he served as member of the Utah territorial legislature for three terms. He died in Fairview, Sanpete County, in 1865 at the age of 79. Isaac and Lucy Morley have left a legacy of faith for their posterity and for all of the Saints.

Chapter 3

"Thy Husband Shall Support Thee in the Church": The Residences of Joseph and Emma Smith

Chronological Summary

- About February 4, 1831—Joseph and Emma Smith arrive in Kirtland and reside in the Whitneys' home
- March 1831—Joseph and Emma move to the Morley farm (first in the Morleys' home and then in their own home)
- September 12, 1831—They move to the Johnsons' farm in Hiram, Ohio
- September 12, 1832—They move to the Whitneys' store
- December 1834—They move into own home just north of the Kirtland Temple

Residences of Joseph and Emma Smith in Kirtland

Over the course of their marriage, Joseph and Emma lived in many locations and in many homes. Each home became a place of revelation, and many served as the headquarters of the Church. While they lived in Kirtland, each of their homes became sacred places because of the significant events and spiritual outpourings that occurred there.

When the Prophet and Emma arrived in Kirtland, the first person they met was Newel K. Whitney. He and his wife, Elizabeth Ann, were among the "Rigdonites," like Isaac and Lucy Morley, who were introduced to the restored gospel by the four Lamanite missionaries. Their lifelong commitment to the Church began with and was foreshadowed by their immediate invitation to the Smiths to live with them, which included giving up their main floor bedroom and sleeping with their children. Joseph recorded that he and Emma "lived in the family of Brother Whitney several weeks, and received every kindness and attention, which could be expected, and especially from Sister [Elizabeth Ann] Whitney."[28] Joseph and Emma lived with them for about a month and a half, from early February to mid-March, before moving to the Morley farm. While living with the Whitneys, Joseph received revelations now found in sections 41–44 of the Doctrine and Covenants. These revelations led to additional revelations later received on the Morley farm. The Whitneys' role in the Restoration is immeasurable, and their hospitality to Joseph and his family allowed the Prophet to receive many important revelations and divine manifestations and played a key role in the organization of the Church.

First Homes

Changing residences and living with others had been a consistent pattern for the newly married Joseph and Emma. Immediately following their January 1827 marriage in Brainbridge near Colesville, New York, and Harmony, Pennsylvania, they traveled to Manchester, New York, to live with Joseph's parents and younger siblings in their frame home. On September 22, 1827, while living in this home, Emma accompanied Joseph during the middle of the night to receive the gold plates and the "interpreters" from the Hill Cumorah.

Immediately following the reception of the plates, Joseph received a steady stream of verbal harassment, and multiple attempts were made to steal the plates. The unsettling nature of that persecution and the nature of the translation process caused Joseph and Emma to move to Harmony, Pennsylvania, to live with Emma's parents. Because of the lack of money, supplies, and transportation, Lucy Mack Smith, Joseph's mother, importuned Martin Harris for a loan to facilitate the move. Due to some initial spiritual experiences relating to the gold plates, he refused to loan the money but instead insisted on giving $50 with no expectation of repayment. This gift helped them to travel to Harmony in December 1827. They traveled in a wagon driven by Emma's brother Alva and accompanied by the gold plates that were concealed in a barrel of beans.

Upon their arrival in Harmony, the Smiths lived with the Hales in their relatively spacious home near the Susquehanna River. However, following Joseph's refusal to allow Emma's father, Isaac, to see the plates, Joseph and Emma were asked to leave, and they took up residence in a home 300 yards to the south that was owned by Emma's brother David. It was here that Joseph continued his efforts to learn how to translate and began the translation of the Book of Mormon with Emma acting as scribe. It was also here that Martin served as scribe from April to June 1828 and where Joseph entrusted Martin with the 116 pages of translation that were eventually lost. It was in this home that Joseph and Emma lost their first child and where Joseph temporarily lost the privilege of translating the Book of Mormon for about three months. Here Joseph later received revelations relating to the loss of the 116-page manuscript that are now sections 3 and part of 10 of the Doctrine and Covenants as well as revelations that became sections 4 and 5.

Oliver Cowdery, while living with Joseph Sr. and Lucy Mack Smith as part of the benefits derived from teaching school, learned of the gold plates and received a witness of their truthfulness. He then traveled with Samuel Smith in March 1829 to Harmony to meet Joseph. He assisted Joseph in securing a mortgage for the property the day before they started translating together—April 7, 1829. During the month of April, Joseph received the revelations now known as sections 6–9 and 11–13, the last of which retells the words of John the Baptist as he conferred the keys of the Aaronic Priesthood on him and Oliver. Section 6 was divine assurance of the Book of Mormon to Oliver, section 7 dealt with the translation of John the Revelator's record, sections 8 and 9 dealt with Oliver's opportunity to translate, and sections 11 and 12 were directed to Hyrum Smith and Joseph Knight Sr., respectively. Although the exact date is not known, the conferral of the keys of the Melchizedek Priesthood by Peter, James, and John likely occurred a short time later (see Doctrine and Covenants 27:12–13; 128:20).[29]

Joseph and Oliver left Harmony on about May 30 when the Lord told them to ask David Whitmer for a place to live and translate in order to escape the intense persecution led by Emma's Methodist uncle. Interestingly, when David arrived at the Smiths', Joseph and Oliver were outside waiting for him. David later stated:

> Oliver told me they knew just when I started, where I put up at night and even the name on the sign board of the hotel where I stayed each night, for he had asked Joseph to look in the seer stone, that he did so, and told him all these particulars, of my journey which Oliver had carefully noted in his book. Oliver asked me where I first met them, when I left home, where I stayed on the road, and the names of the persons keeping the hotels. I could not tell the names but as we returned, I pointed out the several houses where I had stopped, when he pulled out his book and found it to be correct even to the names.[30]

Emma soon followed, and they made their home with the Whitmers where the Book of Mormon translation was completed. While Joseph and Emma lived there, the Book of Mormon copyright and publication contract were secured, the Three and Eight Witnesses saw the plates, and the revelations now recorded as sections 14–19 of the Doctrine and Covenants were received. Sections 14–16 were directed to David, John, and Peter Whitmer Jr., section 17 provided instructions for the Three Witnesses, section 18 was the apostolic charge, and section 19 contains the Savior's description of His suffering in the Garden of Gethsemane. On June 6, while inquiring about when to receive ordination to the office of elder in the Melchizedek Priesthood and bestow the gift of the Holy Ghost (they already had received the keys of that priesthood from Peter, James, and John), "the word of the Lord"[31] commanded

Joseph and Oliver to do so when the previously baptized "brethren" could be gathered together to sustain their ordination (see Doctrine and Covenants 128:21).

Revelations in 1830

Joseph and Emma moved back to Harmony, Pennsylvania, in October while Oliver remained in New York to help supervise the Book of Mormon printing. They returned to the Fayette and Palmyra/Manchester area around the time that the Church of Christ was formally organized on April 6, 1830. In Fayette, the "Articles and Covenants" (section 20) was recorded, and section 21 was received during the organization meeting. Five revelations given for the benefit of five brethren were received that month, later compiled into section 33, and on April 16, a revelation on baptism was received.

Seeking "partial seclusion" (Doctrine and Covenants 24, section heading), Joseph and Emma, along with Oliver and John Whitmer, had returned to their home in Harmony by June where the "visions of Moses" were received and the Bible translation commenced. Three revelations were received in July: various specific directives for the ministry now canonized in section 24; the only revelation in the Doctrine and Covenants dedicated solely for a woman (Emma Smith) in section 25; and the "Law of Common Consent," now section 26. The following month, the first part of section 27 was revealed, with the remainder being revealed the following September.[32]

Early September also saw the Smiths permanently leave their recently paid-for home in Harmony and move to Fayette to live with the Whitmers again. There section 28 was revealed, correcting the Hiram Page seer stone problem and calling Oliver Cowdery to a mission to the Lamanites. Then sections 30 and 32 provided three companions for Oliver later in September and in early October. Section 29—one of the great revelations on the Fall, the Atonement of Christ, and His Second Coming—was revealed before section 28. A revelation for Thomas B. Marsh was received between sections 30 and 32, and revelations for other missionaries, including Orson Pratt, now appear in sections 33 and 34.

During these months, Joseph's parents and younger siblings were discharged from the farm they were renting, the farm they had previously owned. They moved to Waterloo, New York (near Fayette), where Lucy reports they were well received. It was there in December that Sidney Rigdon and Edward Partridge met Joseph and where sections 35 and 36, which were directed to these brethren, were received. Here they also received the command to gather to "the Ohio" in section 37. In early January 1831, during a conference of the Church, the command to gather was reiterated (see section 38). It was again repeated in the revelation given to James Covell shortly after (see section 39), who unfortunately "rejected the word of the Lord" (Doctrine and Covenants 40, section heading). That revelation was the last one received before Joseph and Emma, who was six months pregnant, migrated to Ohio in late January 1831. In the following months, nearly all the New York Saints followed Joseph and Emma and gathered in Ohio. Section 74, one of the Bible interpretation sections, was also received in New York sometime in 1830.

Revelations in Ohio

As discussed previously, Joseph received four sections of the Doctrine and Covenants while living in the Whitneys' home. (Two additional revelations were also later received there, sections 72 and 78.)

In March 1831 Joseph and Emma moved to the Morley farm, living first with the Morleys in their home then later in a home the Church members built for them (see Doctrine and Covenants 41:7). During the six months that Joseph and Emma lived at the Morley farm, thirteen revelations (and possibly section 132) were received. Six of them—sections 57–62—were also received in July and August in Missouri during Joseph's first mission to that area. Sadly, shortly after their births, the twins Emma was carrying while traveling to Ohio passed away. Julia Murdock also passed away that same day while giving birth to twins, whom Joseph and Emma would soon adopt.

In September 1831 Joseph and Emma, along with their adopted twins, moved to Hiram to live with John and Alice (Elsa) Johnson. While living there, Joseph received sixteen revelations that are now recorded in the Doctrine and Covenants. The first revelation, section 66, was received October 1831 and addressed William E. McLellin's five secret questions. The next day Joseph received another revelation, section 65, that concerned priesthood keys and the kingdom of God on the earth.

During a twelve-day period beginning November 1, in which four conferences were held for the purpose of planning the printing of Joseph's revelations, eight sections were received: section 68, instructions for four brethren; section 1, the Lord's preface to the Book of Commandments, the precursor to the Doctrine and Covenants; *The Testimony of the Witnesses to the Book of the Lord's Commandments*; section 67, regarding the hesitancy of some brethren to sign a written testimony of the Book of Commandments; section 133, the Lord's appendix to His revelations; section 69, directions for transporting the revelations to Missouri for printing; a portion of section 107, instructions on the priesthood; and section 70, which directed the establishment of a printing business, or "firm."

In December and January Joseph received sections 71 and 73 in response to anti–Latter-day Saint sentiment in Hiram, and section 75 provided missionary guidance along with the sustaining of the Prophet as President of the High Priesthood. He also received section 76, which revealed the principle of the degrees of glory and further expounded the plan of salvation, and section 77, which provided inspired interpretation of the book of Revelation. Sections 79 and 80 were mission calls, and section 81 was part of the ongoing revelations that unfolded the Lord's will for the presiding quorum of the Church, the First Presidency. Four additional unpublished revelations were also received in Hiram and two canonized in Missouri, sections 82 and 83, during Joseph's second mission to Missouri in April and May. About two-thirds of the Bible translation, a revelatory endeavor in its own right, was also completed in Hiram.

The Smiths next lived in an apartment that the Whitneys provided in the second story of their store from September 1832 to December 1833, where the Prophet received sixteen revelations and finished the Bible translation. Section 84 was received in September, and it comprised another great revelation on priesthood; section 85 was received in November and dealt with problems the Saints had with living the law of consecration in Missouri; section 86 was an inspired interpretation of the parable of the wheat and the tares received in December; and section 87 was a prophecy on war received on Christmas Day. In the later part of December 1832 and January 1833, Joseph received the "Olive Leaf," section 88, and shortly after received the Word of Wisdom, section 89. He also received section 90, which comprised a continuation of the evolving revelations about the First Presidency; section 91, which provided guidance about translating the Apocrypha; and section 92, which provided instruction for Frederick G. Williams. Building on section 88, he received sections 93–96, which portrayed preparatory revelations for the Kirtland Temple, and section 99, a mission call for John Murdock. He also received sections 97, 98, and 101, all dealing with mobocracy in Missouri. Section 100 provided guidance related to Joseph and Sidney Rigdon's mission in Canada, which through a series of divinely orchestrated events led eventually to the gospel being carried to Great Britain.

In 1833 the Church provided another Kirtland home for the Smith family north of the temple site and the Kirtland cemetery. Here Joseph received section 102 the following February, which provided guidance for the creation of the first stake and stake high council, and section 103, which called for the "strength of my house" (verse 21; "Zion's Camp") to go and redeem Zion in Missouri. In April he received section 104, which added divine directions to revelations received previously about the United Order (Firm). In June he received section 105, which gave explanations and directions to Zion's Camp in Missouri. In November he received section 106, and in April 1835, following the constituting of the Quorum of the Twelve Apostles and of the Seventy, he received section 107, directing him in compiling five separate revelations into a single section.

Revelations were also received about or within the Kirtland Temple during this period. Following a short revelation for Lyman Sherman in section 108, the Lord revealed the temple dedicatory prayer the day before the dedication on March 27, 1836. Joseph also received a vision of the Savior in the temple on April 3, 1836, along with visions of Moses, Elias, and Elijah who conferred priesthood keys (see section 110). Section 111 was kind encouragement "notwithstanding [their] follies" (verse 1) when Joseph, Oliver, Sidney, and Hyrum Smith traveled to Salem looking for financial relief from indebtedness from the temple construction and other sources. Section 112 was revealed for

Thomas B. Marsh, President of the Quorum of the Twelve, in the temple and was the last section revealed in Kirtland.

Chapter 4

"Every Man Shall Be a Steward": Unfolding the Law of Consecration and Stewardship

Doctrine and Covenants 38, 41, 42, 48, 51, 54,
and an Unpublished Revelation

Chronological Summary

- January 2, 1831—Initial consecration principles are revealed in New York (Doctrine and Covenants 38)
- About February 4—Joseph and Emma Smith arrive in Kirtland
- February 4—The Saints are instructed to prepare to receive the Lord's law, and Edward Partridge is called as bishop (Doctrine and Covenants 41)
- February 9—Part of "the Law" is revealed (Doctrine and Covenants 42:1–72)
- Between February 9 and 23—The Lord reveals that there is only one at the head of the Church (Doctrine and Covenants 43)

- February 23—The rest of "the Law" is revealed (Doctrine and Covenants 42:73–93)
- Late February—The Saints are instructed to prepare for a conference (Doctrine and Covenants 44)
- June 3–6—The June conference is held (Doctrine and Covenants 52)
- June 8—Algernon Sidney Gilbert is called to serve as a bishop's agent (Doctrine and Covenants 53)
- June 10—The Colesville Saints to move from Thompson to Missouri (Doctrine and Covenants 54)

When the four Lamanite missionaries came to the Morley farm in late October 1830, they found a sizable group of "Rigdonites" known as "The Family," a group committed to the plan of "common stock," which amounted to a communal lifestyle devoted to having "all things common" (Acts 4:32). Sidney Rigdon had become so determined to encourage this communal experiment that he had parted ways with Alexander Campbell over it, resulting in the "Rigdonite" label for those Campbellites who followed Sidney. Lyman Wight's family was the first to move to the Morley farm in February 1830, and they were soon followed by eight more families. Lyman said that the ten families in total experienced "great peace and union" as they were "united both in farming and mechanism, all of which was prosecuted with great vigor. We truly began to feel as if the millennium was close at hand."[33]

All the members of the "Family" accepted the gospel in short order, but when John Whitmer came to Kirtland in January 1831, a month ahead of the Prophet, his characterization of their communal efforts was not so glowing. "The disciples (new members) had all things common and were going to destruction very fast as to temporal things; for they considered from reading the scripture that what belonged to a brother, belonged to any of the brethren. Therefore, they would take each other's clothes and other property and use it without leave which brought on confusion and disappointments, for they did not understand the scripture."[34] Levi Hancock[35] said that while visiting the "Family," Heman Bassett[36] "came to me and took my watch out of my pocket and walked off as though it was his. I thought he would bring it back soon but was disappointed as he sold it. I asked him what he meant by selling my watch. 'Oh,' said he, 'I thought it was all in the family.' I told him I did not like such family doing and I would not bear it."[37] Other "family" problems included individuals moving between the Morley farm and the other "Family" established in nearby Chardon.

When the Prophet and Emma arrived in Kirtland around February 1, "to the joy and satisfaction of the Saints,"[38] they met the recent converts on the Morley farm. It was in this context that the Lord revealed "the more perfect law of the Lord"—that is, the law of consecration that comprised part of the revelation known in general terms as "the Law" found in Doctrine and Covenants 42. (Although not found in the scriptures, the term "law of consecration and stewardship" is often used as a synonym for the "law of consecration.") When it was taught to the "Family," it resulted in the plan of "common stock" being "readily abandoned for the more perfect law of the Lord."[39] Although initially revealed during the month or so that Joseph lived in the Whitneys' home, much of the divine guidance that supported its implementation was received on the Morley farm. It provided not only direction on how to "provide for my Saints . . . in mine own way" (Doctrine and Covenants 104:16) but also a comprehensive economic order that provided for both spiritual and temporal salvation along with the means for financing the work of the kingdom.

Steps Leading Up to the Law of Consecration

As was so often the case in Joseph's revealed leadership, a series of divinely prepared "tutorials" readied the Prophet for the revelatory outpouring that characterized the revealing and directing of the implementation of the law of consecration. Statements translated in 1829, such as King Benjamin's counsel—"For the sake of retaining a remission of your sins . . . I would that ye should impart of your substance to the poor" (Mosiah 4:25)—would have helped him understand the pivotal role that caring for the poor plays in the kingdom of God. Furthermore, as he translated Mormon's depiction of the people following the Savior's visit, he learned "they had all things common among them; therefore there were not rich and poor" (4 Nephi 1:3). Following the organization of The Church of Jesus Christ of Latter-day Saints the next year, Joseph began an inspired revision of the Bible that commenced with the revelations now found in the book of Moses. Among those revelations was a portion of the book of Enoch in which Enoch's people were characterized as "Zion, because they were of one heart . . . and there was no poor among them" (Moses 7:18).

Three consecutive sections in the Doctrine and Covenants directed the New York Saints to move to "the Ohio"—sections 37, 38, and 39. In section 38, the Lord referred to section 37 and foreshadowed His revealing the law of consecration when He said, "I gave unto you the commandment that ye should go to the Ohio; and there I will give unto you my law" (Doctrine and Covenants 38:32).[40] He also taught foundational principles to prepare for receiving and living that law, including the following:

- a reminder that one's possessions are really not her or his because "I have made the earth" (Doctrine and Covenants 38:17) and "the riches of the earth are mine to give" (verse 39);
- an introduction to the notion of stewardship when He spoke of a "land of promise" (verse 18) that He would "give . . . unto you for the land of your inheritance" (verse 19);
- a key to creating interpersonal relationships while living the law in saying, "Let every man esteem his brother as himself" (verse 25);
- a commandment to be united as Enoch's Zion—that is, to "be one; and if ye are not one ye are not mine" (verse 27); and
- a continued emphasis on looking "to the poor and the needy, and administer[ing]" (verse 35) to many of the New York Saints who would be leaving almost all their possessions without adequate financial renumeration in their move to Ohio.

The next two steps in the unfolding of the law of consecration occurred within a few days following Joseph and Emma's arrival in Kirtland, when they were invited to take up temporary residence in the home of Newel K. and Elizabeth Ann Whitney. In that home, the Lord commanded that a group of "elders of my church . . . shall assemble yourselves together" to "receive my law" (Doctrine and Covenants 41:2–3).[41] Then, following the direction that "my servant Joseph Smith, Jun., should have a house built in which to live and translate" (verse 7)—which was fulfilled two months later on the Morley farm—He revealed the priesthood office that would direct the implementation of consecration and the first man to fill it: "I have called my servant Edward Partridge; and . . . he should be ordained a bishop unto the church" (Doctrine and Covenants 41:9). (A summary of the life of Edward and Lydia Partridge appears in the footnotes.)[42]

The Law

Prior to the divinely directed organization of various standing leadership councils—the First Presidency, the Quorum of the Twelve Apostles, quorum presidencies, high councils, and the like—the Lord instructed Joseph to create ad hoc councils to serve functions similar to standing ones, thus the direction in Doctrine and Covenants 41 to "the elders" to "assemble yourselves together" (verse 2). On February 9, 1831, Joseph assembled twelve elders in the Whitney home, and together they sought a fulfillment of the promise that "by the prayer of your faith ye shall receive my law" (Doctrine and Covenants 41:3). This meeting saw the beginning of a series of revelations that continued through February 23. The chronology and organization of those revelations differs to some extent from that which appears in the current edition of the Doctrine and Covenants, a reflection of the Lord's "line upon line" means of revealing His will and of the inspired process of revelation compilation that characterized their publication. Elements of the law of consecration appear in all of them along with numerous other divine directives and thrilling doctrines, some of which appear in other chapters in this book. On February 9 most of the revelation that is now known as Doctrine and Covenants 42:1–73 was revealed. It appears that the revelations constituting sections 43 and 44 came next, although the exact dates they were revealed are not known. On February 23 Joseph met with seven elders as a continuation of the February 9 meeting, and the contents of the remaining verses of section 42 were revealed.

The revelatory experience that characterized the February 9 meeting seems to have been structured by specific questions or implied questions the brethren were seeking answers for. Indeed, some of the initial recordings of "the Law" include these questions, although with some wording differences depending upon the recorder:

1. "Shall the Church come together unto one place or continue in separate establishments?" (answered in verses 1–10)

2. "[What is] the Law regulating the Church in her present situation till the time of her gathering?" (answered in verses 11–69)

3. "How are the elders to dispose of their families while they are proclaiming repentance or are otherwise engaged in the service of the Church?" (answered in verses 70–73)

4. "How far is it the will of the Lord that we should have dealing with the world & how we should conduct our dealings with them?" (answer not included in the published revelation)

5. "What preparations we shall make for our brethren from the East & where & how?" (answer not included in the published revelation but discussed below)

Elements of the law of consecration are found in the Lord's responses to questions 2–5. First, in recognition of the previously revealed principle that "the riches of the earth are mine to give" (Doctrine and Covenants 38:39), the Lord directed the Saints to "consecrate of thy properties" (all possessions, land or otherwise) through a legally-binding "covenant and deed which cannot be broken" (Doctrine and Covenants 42:30). The "bishop of my church," or others "he shall appoint," were to act as receiving agents to whom the consecrated properties were to be "laid before" (verse 31). After reiterating the notion that the consecrated properties "cannot be taken from the church," the Lord then said that "every man shall be made . . . a steward over his own property" (the portion of his or her original possessions deeded back to him or her) or "that which he has received by consecration" (additional items and/or property beyond his or her original consecration provided by the consecration of others), "as much as is sufficient for himself and family" (verse 32). The property deeded back became one's "stewardship," things that were leased individually and not communally.

Speaking of the consecration of others providing for those who didn't have sufficient for their needs, the revelation stated, "If there shall be properties . . . more than is necessary for their support after this first consecration, which is a residue, . . . it shall be kept to administer to those who have not . . . that every man who has need may be amply supplied" (verse 33). This residue was to "be kept in my storehouse, to be administered to the poor and the needy, as shall be appointed by . . . the bishop and his council" (verse 34; "council"[43] refers to the council formed by Joseph and his counselors who were soon to be named, John Corrill[44] and Isaac Morley). A few verses later, the Lord reiterated, "If thou obtainest more than that which would be for thy support, thou shalt give it into my storehouse" (verse 54). Thus, a pillar of today's welfare system was revealed: the bishops' storehouse.

The residue in the storehouse was also earmarked for other sacred purposes: "purchasing lands for the public benefit of the church, building houses of worship, and building up of the New Jerusalem . . . hereafter to be revealed" (verse 35). Land purchasing not only referred to the purchase of lands for general Church use but for habitations for those obeying the command to gather and couldn't otherwise afford to purchase property on their own, which means land became part of the storehouse system.

The Lord addressed some of the challenges that arose among the "Family." Speaking of those who didn't carry their weight, so to speak, He commanded, "Thou shalt not be idle; for he that is idle shall not eat the bread nor wear the garments of the laborer" (verse 42). To correct the problem of a lack of commitment to the whole, or moving from one group of consecrated Saints to another, the Lord said, "Thou shalt stand in the place of thy stewardship" (verse 53). Levi Hancock was probably relieved when he heard that "thou shalt not take thy brother's garment; thou shalt pay for that which thou shalt receive" (verse 54).

Another function of the storehouse was to support those who served in the Church full-time. When Edward Partridge was called to be the first bishop (see section 41) the Lord added that he was to "leave his merchandise [Edward was a very successful "hatter"] and to spend all his time in the labors of the church" (Doctrine and Covenants 41:9). The Lord then said, "The bishop, also, shall receive his support, or a just remuneration for all his services in the church" (Doctrine and Covenants 42:73). The "also" refers to those "elders or high priests ["high priests" was added later] who [were] appointed to assist the bishop as counselors," who were "to have their families supported out of the property which is consecrated to the bishop" (Doctrine and Covenants 42:71).

Procuring Lands

One of the questions that structured the revelatory experience that produced "the Law" was accompanied by an answer that was not recorded in section 42—"What preparations we shall make for our brethren from the East & where & how?" The Lord answered, "There shall be as many appointed as must needs be necessary to assist the Bishop in obtaining places that they may be together as much as can be and is directed by the Holy Spirit and every family shall have places that they may live by themselves and every Church [branch] shall be organized in as close bodies as they can be in consequence of the enemy!"[45] Given this answer—along with wording in "the Law" regarding his responsibility for "the properties of my church" (verse 32) and to "administer to the poor and needy" (verse 34), and the fact that "there was no preparation made for the reception of the Saints from the east"—it's not surprising that a month later, when "the time drew near for the brethren from the State of New York to arrive at Kirtland, Ohio . . ., the bishop [was] anxious to know something concerning the matter, therefore the Lord spake unto Joseph Jr Smith Jr. as follows."[46] What the Lord spake to Joseph is recorded in Doctrine and Covenants 48, the fourth section revealed on the Morley farm.

The Lord said that "inasmuch as ye have lands," referring to surplus lands in the storehouse, "ye shall impart to the eastern brethren" (Doctrine and Covenants 48:2). In the next verse, the Lord authorized Edward Partridge and others called to assist him to purchase lands "in those regions round about . . . for it must be necessary that they have places to live for the present time" (verse 3). Thus began the practice of procuring lands as the Saints gathered to Kirtland; Jackson, Clay, Caldwell, and Daviess counties in Missouri; and Nauvoo, Illinois, and surrounding areas.

Curious wording commences the revelation: "Ye should remain for the present time in your places of abode" (verse 1). John Whitmer also wrote along with his commentary about the coming of the eastern Saints, "And some had supposed that it [meaning Kirtland] was the place of gathering even the place of the New Jerusalem spoken of in the Book of Mormon, according to the visions and revelations received in the last days."[47] Therefore, the Lord said, "It must needs be necessary that ye save all the money that ye can, . . . [that] ye may be enabled to purchase land for an inheritance, even the city" (verse 4). The next verses indicated that "there are to be certain men appointed, and to them it shall be given to know the place, or to them it shall be revealed. And they shall be appointed to purchase the lands, and to make a commencement to lay the foundation of the city; and then shall ye begin to be gathered with your families" (verses 5–6). As will be discussed more fully later in this book, this other gathering place was none other than Jackson County, Missouri—Zion, the New Jerusalem.

An Unpublished Revelation Involving the Sharing of Lands Owned by the Saints

Part of the storehouse system envisioned by the Lord included the Kirtland Saints using their lands to provide homes for the fairly large groups of New York Saints who began arriving in May 1831. Isaac Morley was very generous in this regard, and in fact, more New York Saints lived on his property than on any other. Another generous Saint was Frederick G. Williams, and issues involving the sharing of his property were the subject of an unpublished revelation given in between the days when the revelations now found in sections 50 and 51 were revealed.

Frederick exchanged some land he owned in Warrensville, Ohio, for some land in Kirtland owned by Isaac Moore (not to be confused with Isaac Morley). Isaac's was worth $500 more than Frederick's due to structures existing on the property, so Frederick agreed to pay the difference. Although the transaction had taken place by early 1830, Moore had not vacated his Kirtland property by May 1831 despite having received $100 of the $500 he was owed. Moore's motivation for not moving may have been monetary, religious, or both. He was a Campbellite leader in the Kirtland area who had aggressively resisted the preaching of the four Lamanite missionaries. To complicate matters, Frederick had joined the Lamanite missionaries as they departed Kirtland for Missouri in November 1830. In fact, a letter from Frederick to his wife in April may have instigated the questions that led to the revelations. Frederick's letter included the instruction "that respecting that suit at Law there can be nothing done on their part more till August term."⁴⁸

Further complications arose when Joseph Smith Sr., who was living in the Morleys' home, was joined by seven other members of his family, including his wife, Lucy. It was anticipated that the Smiths would move on to the Williams' property in Kirtland. Therefore, the Lord indicated that the Williams should "let the bargain stand that ye have made concerning these two farms until it be so fulfilled."⁴⁹ The Lord referred to Isaac Moore as "thine advisory" and said that no more money should be paid to him until "the contract be fulfilled" (i.e., until he moved out). He then said, "Let my servant Joseph [Smith Sr.] and his family go into the house . . . and let my servant Ezra [Thayre] board with him." He instructed that a house should be erected for Ezra and that Joseph Sr. should "govern the things of the farm & provide for the families" apparently with Ezra's assistance. Indeed, in a conference held on October 10, 1831, Joseph Sr. and Ezra were rebuked for taking an "unwise course."⁵⁰ The conference directed that "Br Frederick G Williams' family be provided with a comfortable dwelling by this Church," suggesting that Joseph Sr.'s and Ezra's "unwise course" was not providing adequately for the Williams family. However, Lucy Mack Smith talked about this home in her history but made no comment about the rebuke: "On this farm my family were all established with this arrangement that we were to cultivate the farm and the produce was to be applied to the support of our families and the use of persons who were came to the place and had no acquaintances there."⁵¹ Perhaps motivated by a cessation of payments, Isaac Moore moved to Warrensville in late May.

Foreshadowing Ezra's future mission call to Missouri (see Doctrine and Covenants 52), the Lord also said, "Let my servant Ezra humble himself and at the conference meeting [in June on the Morley farm— see Doctrine and Covenants 44:1–2] he shall be ordained unto power from on high [a reference to his receiving the office of high priest] and he shall go from thence (if he be obedient unto my commandments) and proclaim my Gospel unto the western regions with my Servants that must go forth even unto the borders of the Lamanit[e]s."⁵²

The recording of this unpublished revelation also includes a question—"What shall the Brethren do with their money[?]"—referring to the Saints arriving from Palmyra. It tells them to acquire land but also save "money that it may be consecrated to purchase lands in the west for an everlasting inheritance," another reference to the New Jerusalem in Jackson County.

Aiding the Colesville Saints:
Sections 51 and 54 on the Morley Farm

Two more revelations were given shortly after the unpublished one and were also concerned with providing land for migrating Saints using the principles of the law of consecration. They dealt specifically with the sixty or so members from Broome and Chenango counties in New York, who comprised the Colesville Branch, and Leman Copley, a relatively wealthy new convert who had previously been a "Shaker" or "Shaking Quaker" (i.e., a member of the United Society of Believers in Christ's Second Appearing). That branch had originally been presided over by Hyrum Smith who had taken up residence in the area, but when Hyrum left to take his own family and his parents and younger siblings to Ohio, Newel Knight, the son of Joseph Sr. and Polly Knight, was appointed in his stead. Newel led the branch members in leaving for Ohio in mid-April 1831, traveling by wagon train, canal boats, and across Lake Erie where their trip was delayed for over a week by an ice blockage.

Newel wrote that when they arrived in the Kirtland area on May 16, "it was advised that the Colesville Branch remain together and go to [a] neighboring town called Thompson [22 miles east of Kirtland] as a man by the name [Leman] Copley owned a considerable tract of land there which he offered to let the brethren occupy."[53] Leman had previously "requested Brother Joseph and Sidney [Rigdon] . . . live with him and he would furnish them houses and provisions" (Doctrine and Covenants 41, section heading). Instead, the Lord directed that their home be constructed on the Morley farm.[54] But in March, Joseph and Joseph Knight Sr.—a Colesville Saint who, along with his wife, Polly, had accompanied the Prophet to Thompson—apparently inquired into the possibility of the Colesville Saints settling there (instead of Joseph and Sidney). Leman accepted the idea.

The specific arrangements for dividing up consecrated property for settlement according to the law of consecration was the purview of the bishop (see Doctrine and Covenants 42:31), and Edward Partridge sought for divine guidance as to how "to organize this people according to [God's] laws" (Doctrine and Covenants 51:1–2). Clarifying the apportioning of stewardships, the Lord said, "Every man [was to be] equal according to his family, according to his circumstances and his wants and needs" (Doctrine and Covenants 51:3). The judgement regarding the amount of property deeded back to the donor was to be something of a mutual endeavor. Joseph wrote in 1833:

> Every man must be his own judge how much he should receive and how much he should suffer to remain in the hands of the Bishop. I speak of those who consecrate more than they need for the support of themselves and their families. The matter of consecration must be done by the mutual consent of both parties; for to give the Bishop power to say how much every man shall have, and he be obliged to comply with the Bishop's judgment, is giving to the Bishop more power than a king has; and upon the other hand, to let every man say how much he needs, and the Bishop be obliged to comply with his judgment, is to throw Zion into confusion, and make a slave of the Bishop. The fact is, there must be a balance or equilibrium of power, between the Bishop and the people, and thus harmony and good will may be preserved among you.[55]

Each stewardship was to be conveyed by a legal deed, "a writing that shall secure unto him his portion" (Doctrine and Covenants 51:4). Such "writings," at least ones used in Missouri two years later, consisted of a consecration deed on the left side and a stewardship deed on the right. The left-hand side granted the property to "Edward Partridge, . . . bishop [of] said church," included a description of the property, and stated that a named person covenanted forever "to release all" their "right and interest to the above described property."[56] The right-hand side of the document read, "Be it known that I, Edward Partridge . . . bishop of the church of Christ, . . . have leased, and by these presents do lease unto [individual's name written by hand] of Jackson County, and state of Missouri, a member of said church, the following described piece or parcel of land . . . [description of property written by hand] . . . to have and to hold the above property." Levi Jackman's deed conveyed "sundry articles of furniture valued thirty-seven dollars, also two beds, bedding, and feathers valued forty-four dollars fifty cents, also three axes and other tools valued eleven dollars and twenty five cents"—all he possessed. In return, received a parcel of land, "sundry articles of furniture . . . two beds bedding and feathers . . . also three axes and other tools."[57]

The document went on to indicate that if the agreed party lost his or her membership, he or she would "forfeit all claim to the above described leased and loaned property." This forfeiture aligned with the original wording of Doctrine and Covenants 51:4–5. However, because it was unconstitutional for a religious organization to deprive an individual of his or her property, verse 5 was changed to read that a former member "shall not retain the gift [the original consecration], but shall only have claim on that portion that is deeded [leased back] unto him." The Prophet later wrote, "On the subject of giving deeds, and receiving contributions from brethren, I have nothing further to say on the subject than to recommend that you make yourselves acquainted with the commandments of the Lord, and the laws of the state, and govern yourselves accordingly."[58]

The original commandments associated with the law of consecration involved lease agreements. As a result of varied legalities and Joseph's inspired revision of section 51, Bishop Partridge was instructed to deed land to the Saints in "fee simple," a legal term referring to absolute and permanent ownership. Thus, the Saints were to take ownership of their stewardships in a legal sense. However, the Lord had told the Saints earlier in section 38 that "the riches of the earth are mine to give" (verse 32) and continued to emphasize His ultimate ownership as Creator in subsequent revelations. For example, three years later while the Church was still headquartered in Kirtland, the Lord said, "I, the Lord, . . . built the earth, my very handiwork; and all things therein are mine. . . . A commandment I give unto you concerning your stewardship. . . . All these properties are mine . . . and if the properties are mine, then ye are stewards" (Doctrine and Covenants 104:14, 54–56).

The Lord further reaffirmed two previously revealed elements from section 42. First, the bishop was to "appoint a storehouse unto this church" so that commodities "which are more needful for the wants of the people, be kept in the hands of the bishop" (Doctrine and Covenants 51:13). Second, to guide His direction that the bishop receive "just remuneration for all his [full-time] services in the church" (Doctrine and Covenants 42:73), the Lord said, "Let [the bishop] reserve unto himself for his own wants, and for the wants of his family, as he shall be employed in doing this business" (Doctrine and Covenants 51:14). Interestingly, the Lord characterized participation in the law of consecration as a "privilege" because He Himself was an equal participant: "I consecrate unto them this land" (Doctrine and Covenants 51:16). So the Colesville Saints "all went to work and made fence and planted and sowed the fields," making a living for themselves while making improvements on Leman's property.[59]

The Lord foreshadowed the temporary nature of this arrangement, however, when He indicated that it was to be "for a little season until I, the Lord, shall provide for them otherwise, and command them to go hence. . . . Wherefore let them act upon this land as for years" (Doctrine and Covenants 51:16–17). And temporary it was.

Leman accompanied Sidney Rigdon and Parley P. Pratt to preach the Shakers, his former religious colleagues, in a settlement near Cleveland (see section 49, revealed May 7, 1831, and chapter 12 of this book). Although polite at first, contentions eventually arose and the Shakers rejected the message, which seemed to have had a negative effect on Leman. He returned to the Shaker settlement, where it seems he tried to patch things up with his former friends. He then returned to his farm and brought along the Shaker leader, Ashbel Kitchell, which resulted in a rather antagonistic confrontation causing Leman to break "his covenant to consecrate his large farm as a place of inheritance for the Saints arriving from Colesville" (Doctrine and Covenants 54, section heading). Joseph Knight's son, Joseph Knight Jr., remembered, "We had to leave his [Copley's] farm and pay sixty dollars damage," ironically, for the improvements they made in "fitting up his houses and planting his ground."[60]

This difficult situation prompted Newel Knight to travel to the Morley farm to seek guidance from the Prophet. He arrived just before the June conference in which the Lord directed several brethren to travel to Missouri (see Doctrine and Covenants 52 and chapter 9 of this book). In his history, John Whitmer suggested that Leman's reneging affected more than just the Colesville Saints: "At this time the Church at Thompson Ohio was involved in difficulty, because of the rebellion of Leman Copley, who would not do as he had previously agreed which thing confused the whole church and finally the Lord spake unto Joseph Smith Jr the prophet."[61] Newel continued, "As I had come to see brother Joseph concerning our position in Thompson, he enquired of the Lord and received the following revelation [section 54]."[62] This revelation moved beyond the somewhat general direction regarding gathering, found in section 52, to the specific instruction for the Colesville Saints to gather to Missouri.

In the revelation, the Lord directed Newel to "stand fast in the office whereunto I have appointed you" (Doctrine and Covenants 54:2), referring to his call to serve a mission to Missouri (see Doctrine and Covenants 52:32). It also appears that some of his branch members may have also been somewhat to blame for being ejected from Leman's property, for the Lord said, "Let them repent of all their sins" (Doctrine and Covenants 54:3). Then the Lord referred to "the covenant which they made unto me" (the law of consecration) as being "broken" and therefore "void and of none effect" (verse 4), leading to his instruction to "flee the land, lest your enemies come upon you . . . and appoint whom you will to be your leader" (verse 7). Speaking more specifically of their destination, the Lord directed, "You shall take your journey into the regions westward, unto the land of Missouri, unto the borders of the Lamanites" (verse 8). Upon hearing the Prophet utter these words, Newel remarked, "We now understood that this [Ohio] was not the land of our inheritance—the land of promise, for it was made known in a revelation, that Missouri was the place chosen for the gathering of the Church, and several were called to lead the way to that state." Thus, the Colesville Saints were among the first to try to practice the law of consecration in Ohio and became the first to try to do so in Missouri.

As a foreshadowing of future events, the Lord cautioned, "Be patient in tribulation until I come" (verse 10)—perhaps an illusion to the future difficulties that were to be had in Jackson County, then Clay County, and then in Caldwell and Daviess counties in Missouri.

One more revelation dealt with an aspect of the Colesville Saints' move to Missouri. As noted above, Newel Knight was called on a mission with Ezra Thayre to Missouri (see Doctrine and Covenants 52), a call that was reiterated in section 54, as explained above. Unfortunately, Ezra had not been faithful to the commandment to adequately assist the Smith and Williams families. Also, Ezra may have been the one who paid the $100 toward satisfying a portion of the debt on the property in an attempt to obtain some sort of title to a portion of it, which explains why the June 15 revelation declared that Ezra "must repent of his pride, and of his selfishness, and obey the former commandment which I have given him concerning the place upon which he lives . . . [and] there shall no divisions be made upon the land" (Doctrine and Covenants 56:8–9). These temporal matters distracted him from his call to Missouri revealed in the May 15 unpublished revelation and in section 52. Therefore, the Lord said he could either go on his mission to Missouri or "otherwise he shall receive the money which he has paid, and shall leave the place, and shall be cut off out of my Church" (Doctrine and Covenants 56:10).

Ezra's disobedience resulted in the Lord "revok[ing] the command-ment . . . given unto . . . Thomas B. Marsh and Ezra Thayre [to serve as mission companions to Missouri], and [giving] a new command-ment unto . . . Thomas" to go "to the land of Missouri" with "my servant Selah J. Griffin" (verse 5). This new command also caused the Lord to "revoke the commandment which was given unto . . . Selah Griffin" and "because of the stiffneckedness of my people which are in Thompson" (the Colesville Saints), the commandment given to Newel Night, who had been assigned as his companion (see verse 6). Then Newel was assigned to "remain with them . . . and be led by him to the land which I have appointed" (verse 7, referring to Missouri), thus allowing him to maintain his Colesville Branch leadership position as the Colesville Saints had hoped. It's no surprise the Lord took the op-portunity to highlight key elements of the law of consecration at this point: "You have many things to do and to repent of . . . because you seek to counsel in your own ways. And your hearts are satisfied. . . . Wo unto you rich men, that will not give your substance to the poor. . . . Wo unto you poor men, whose hearts are not broken, whose spirits are not contrite, and whose bellies are not satisfied, and whose hands are not stayed from laying hold upon other men's goods. . . . But blessed are the poor who are pure in heart, whose hearts are broken, and whose spirits are contrite" (verses 14, 16–18).

Chapter 5

"SEEK YE EARNESTLY THE BEST GIFTS": DEALING WITH FALSE GIFTS AND DOCTRINES

Doctrine and Covenants 42, 43, 46, 49, and 50

Chronological Summary

- February 9, 1831—Part of "the Law" is revealed (Doctrine and Covenants 42:1–72)
- Between February 9 and 23—The Lord reveals that there is only one at the head of the Church (Doctrine and Covenants 43)
- February 23—The rest of "the Law" is revealed (Doctrine and Covenants 42:73–93)
- Late February—The Saints are instructed to prepare for a conference (Doctrine and Covenants 44)
- About March 7—Joseph receives a revelation in response to "false reports and foolish stories" being published (Doctrine and Covenants 45)

- March 8—The Joseph Smith Translation of the New Testament begins
- About March 8—The Lord provides instruction about Church governance, conducting meetings, and spiritual gifts (Doctrine and Covenants 46)
- March 8—John Whitmer is called as the Church Historian and recorder (Doctrine and Covenants 47)
- May 7—Leman Copley and others are instructed to preach to the Shakers (Doctrine and Covenants 49)
- May 9—Joseph receives a revelation about teaching by the Spirit and dealing with false spirits (Doctrine and Covenants 50)
- June 3–6—The June conference is held (Doctrine and Covenants 52)

The four Lamanite missionaries witnessed great growth in the Church in the three weeks they visited northeast Ohio in October and November 1830. Accounts vary as to the exact number, but several indicate that there were over 100 baptisms, and Parley P. Pratt, one of the four missionaries, recorded 127.[63] After the missionaries continued west to the "borders by the Lamanites" (Doctrine and Covenants 28:9), the Church continued to grow in Ohio, reaching 400 members by the time Joseph and Emma Smith arrived in Kirtland just two and a half months later.

With this rapid growth came challenges. First was the issue of leaving old beliefs behind. The restorationist perspective held by Sidney Rigdon and others that rejected mainstream Protestantism meant that these new converts already believed many of the doctrines taught by the four missionaries, so doctrinal differences were hardly an obstacle to conversion. But as the Restoration unfolded and doctrines were revealed that contradicted many previously held beliefs, many converts had varying degrees of difficulty in accepting them, and some even left the Church as a result. Second, the Saints struggled with spiritual discernment. The message of the doctrine of Christ, which included the authorized bestowal of the gift of the Holy Ghost with its attending spiritual gifts, resonated with many who not only valued but enjoyed spiritual manifestations prior to conversion. Teaching the Saints about spiritual discernment became a major challenge that Joseph Smith had to take on when he came to Ohio. Indeed, several revelations came as a result of his importuning the Lord for help in this regard. These revelations were given to help the Saints not be "seduced by evil spirits, or doctrines of devils, or the commandments of men" (Doctrine and Covenants 46:7).

The Priesthood of All Believers: Section 43

One reason for the misunderstanding of spiritual gifts may have stemmed from the new converts' confusion over two ideas that they coupled together: (1) the gift of the Holy Ghost received by all members and (2) the notion of a universal priesthood (i.e., the priesthood of all believers, a foundational tenet of Protestantism). It is not surprising that, in the midst of the great American experiment in democracy, a democratic notion such as a universal priesthood would become so prominent. However, it was proclaimed long before the idea of an American nation ever entered the minds of the Europeans. John Calvin and Martin Luther both espoused the notion, and Martin said, "That the pope or bishop anoints, makes tonsures, ordains, consecrates, or dresses differently from the laity, may make a hypocrite or an idolatrous oil-painted icon, but it in no way makes a Christian or spiritual human being. In fact, we are all consecrated priests through Baptism, as St. Peter in 1 Peter 2[:9] says, 'You are a royal priesthood and a priestly kingdom,' and Revelation [5:10], 'Through your blood you have made us into priests and kings.'"[64]

This notion of a universal priesthood did not preclude leadership, organization, or a ministerial order (i.e., individuals holding some authority, albeit mere localized recognition in many instances) to preach, perform ordinances, or otherwise serve congregations. Whether receiving such authority by ordination, licensure, or some other means, common to all was an individual's sense of being called independent of ecclesiastical input. In many instances, training would be provided and then some sort of formal recognition, but especially in the new America, a preacher might simply feel a sense of authority simply by obtaining a following. The new Ohio Saints were not immune to taking upon themselves without proper authority varied ecclesiastical roles because of this Protestant tradition, particularly because they had received the gift of the Holy Ghost. To help the Saints understand the ecclesiastical order of His Church, the Lord revealed to them "the Law."

"The Law" contained in Doctrine and Covenants 42 that directed the economic order of the kingdom of God—"the law of consecration and stewardship"—also provided important ecclesiastical direction. In it the Lord said, "It shall not be given to anyone to go forth to preach my gospel, or to build up my church" (verse 11) unless two conditions were satisfied. First, he needed to "be ordained by someone who has authority." This notion was not necessarily unique, but in a religion established after nearly two millennia of apostasy, that person "who has authority" would have had to be authorized by those who were given actual divine authority by heavenly messengers (i.e., "been regularly ordained by the heads of the church" [verse 11]). Second, it was to be "known to the church that he has authority" (verse 11).

The new Ohio Saints did not have access to the New York revelations that had made these conditions abundantly clear. The role of ordination by someone who was authorized to ordain others was revealed in the "Articles and Covenants," the first "handbook of instructions" now known as section 20. As Doctrine and Covenants 20:60 states, "Every elder, priest, teacher, or deacon is to be ordained according to the gifts and callings of God unto him, and he is to be ordained by the power of the Holy Ghost, which is in the one who ordains him." Furthermore, "no person is to be ordained to any office in this church . . . without the vote of that church" (verse 65). Three months later the Lord had further clarified that "all things shall be done by common consent in the church" (Doctrine and Covenants 26:2).

Despite these New York revelations and the guidance found in "the Law," a challenge arose that reflected the combined influence of a belief in a universal priesthood and the fact that all members were entitled to revelation. A new convert, commonly known in Church history as "Mrs. Hubble," who was believed to possess significant spiritual gifts caused "some members of the Church" to be "disturbed by people making false claims as revelators" (Doctrine and Covenants 43, section heading). Her name was likely Laura Fuller Hubbell.[65] Laura had emigrated from New York with her husband, Adoniram, in 1819 and first settled in Chagrin (now Willoughby) where Adoniram established a hat shop. The shop burned down in 1827, after which the

Hubbles moved to Newburg near Cleveland where they raised three young children.

In describing Laura's influence when she came to Kirtland, Joseph said she was "a woman . . . with great pretentions to revealing commandments, laws and other curious matters."[66] John Whitmer recorded that she "professed to be a prophetess of the Lord and professed to have many revelations," and because she appeared "sanctimonious," some Saints "were not able to detect her in her hypocrisy."[67] Ezra Booth added that she "so ingratiated herself into the esteem and favor of some of the Elders, that they received her, as a person commissioned to act a conspicuous part of Mormonizing the world."[68] Her revelatory claims bore witness of the Book of Mormon but also indicated "that she should become a teacher in the Church of Christ."[69] At issue, therefore, was whether individual members could be directed by their own divine revelation to be ordained teachers and thus receive authority to direct Church administration.

Finding it "necessary to inquire of the Lord,"[70] the Prophet received this revelation "that the Saints might not be deceived."[71] The Lord first stated that the Church had just "received a commandment for a law unto my church," referring to Doctrine and Covenants 42:1–69, "through him whom I have appointed unto you to receive commandments and revelations from my hand" (Doctrine and Covenants 43:1), and that "there is none other appointed unto you to receive commandments and revelations until he be taken" (verse 2). The Ohio Saints were probably not aware that on the day the Church was organized, the Lord had similarly stated that the Church "shall give heed unto all his [Joseph Smith's] words and commandments . . . as if from mine own mouth" (Doctrine and Covenants 21:4–5). They may also not have been aware that a problem similar to the Hubble challenge had arisen the previous September when Hiram Page claimed to be receiving revelation for the Church about the location of Zion, to which the Lord said, "No one shall be appointed to receive commandments and revelations in this church excepting my servant Joseph Smith, Jun." (Doctrine and Covenants 28:2).

This reiteration in section 43 of the order of Church governance might actually be considered part of "the Law" because it was revealed in between the two "official" days when all of "the Law" was revealed and because the Lord Himself said, "This shall be a law unto you" (Doctrine and Covenants 43:5). The Saints were not to "receive . . . the teachings of any that shall come before you as revelations or commandments" in order that they "may not be deceived, that you may know they are not of me" (verses 5–6). He then made the fulfillment of the Saints' desires for the "glories" and the "mysteries of the kingdom" contingent on upholding Joseph "by the prayer of faith" and by providing "for him food and raiment, and whatsoever thing he needeth" (verses 12–13).

The Lord then reiterated this matter of "Church polity" (Doctrine and Covenants 43, section heading) to the Hubble problem by repeating what He had said in "the Law" (see Doctrine and Covenants 42:11), stating, "He that is ordained of me shall come in at the gate and be ordained *as I have told you before*, to teach those revelations which you have received and shall receive through him whom I have appointed" (Doctrine and Covenants 43:7). Again, this latter direction reiterated "the Law," which directed that "teachers of this church shall teach the principles of my gospel, which are in the Bible and the Book of Mormon. . . . And they shall observe the covenants and church articles [a reference to section 20] to do them, and these shall be their teachings" (Doctrine and Covenants 42:12–13), adding that the proper role for divine revelation for a teacher was to teach these principles "as they shall be directed by the Spirit" (verse 13).

Ezra Booth said that soon after the incident, Laura "returned to the place from whence she came."[72] Her family left Newburg in 1835 to settle in Michigan where Laura died in 1850.

Religious Enthusiasm and Ecstatic Spiritual Demonstrations: Section 46

Another difficulty brought on by the inclusion of previous religious traditions among the new converts in Ohio was the practice of "religious enthusiasm"—that is, engaging in very dramatic and demonstrative behaviors supposedly inspired by the Holy Ghost. These behaviors were particularly prominent among certain branches of the Baptists and the Methodists, although other branches of those denominations were vigorous in their opposition to them. When converts came from the Baptist and Methodist branches practicing enthusiasm, they brought their spiritual practices with them, which brought a great deal of judgment from those who opposed the Church. One article in a local newspaper portrayed rather graphic descriptions of religious enthusiasm among the Saints after the four Lamanite missionaries left Ohio and Sidney Rigdon went to New York to meet the Prophet:

> Immediately after Mr. R[igdon] and the four pretended proph-
> ets left Kirtland, a scene of the wildest enthusiasm was exhibited,
> chiefly, however, among the young people; they would fall, as with-
> out strength, roll upon the floor, and, so mad were they that even
> the females were seen on a cold winter day, lying under the bare
> canopy of heaven, with no couch or pillow but the fleecy snow. At
> other times they exhibited all the apish actions imaginable, making
> grimaces both horrid and ridiculous, creeping upon their hands and
> feet, &c. Sometimes, in these exercises the young men would rise
> and play before the people, going through all the Indian maneu-
> vers of knocking down, scalping, ripping open, and taking out the
> bowels. At other times, they would start and run several furlongs,
> then get upon stumps and preach to imagined congregations, bap-
> tize ghosts, &c. At other times, they are taken with a fit of jabbering
> after which they neither understood themselves nor anybody else,
> and this they call speaking foreign languages by divine inspiration.
> Again the young men are seen running over the hills in pursuit, they
> say, of balls of fire which they see flying through the air.[73]

John Whitmer took notice of the odd behaviors when he arrived in Kirtland a month before the Prophet, indicating that "the enemy of all righteous had got hold of some of those who professed to be his fol-lowers, because they had not sufficient knowledge to detect him in all his devices."[74] He went on to list what he observed in ways that aligned with Eber Howe's depiction:

> Some had visions and could not tell what they saw. Some would
> fancy to themselves that they had the sword of Laban and would
> wield it as expert as a light dragoon, some would act like an Indian
> in the act of scalping, some would slide or scoot and [on] the floor,
> with the rapidity of a serpent, which the[y] termed sailing in the boat
> to the Lamanites, preaching the gospel. And many other vain and

foolish maneuvers that are unseeming, and unprofitable to mention. Thus the devil blinded the eyes of some good and honest disciples.[75]

The revelation now recorded in Doctrine and Covenants 46 addresses religious enthusiasm. The Lord first indicated the source of these gifts as "evil spirits, or doctrine of devils, or the commandments of men" (verse 7). Adding a caution "lest ye are deceived; and that ye may not be deceived" (verse 8), He indicated that the antidote was to "seek ye earnestly the best gifts, always remembering for what they are given"—that is, "for the benefit of those who love me and keep all my commandments, and him that seeketh so to do . . . and not for a sign that they may consume it upon their lusts" (verse 9). Then, to be clear, the Lord provided a list of "what those gifts are" that He gives "unto the church . . . for there are many gifts, and to every man is given a gift. . . . To some is given one, and to some is given another, that all may be profited thereby" (verses 10–12). He added that the "discerning of spirits" was to be particularly utilized by "the bishop . . . and unto such as God shall appoint and ordain to watch over the Church . . . lest there shall be any among you professing and yet be not of God" (verse 27).

Armed with this revelation, the Prophet had at least some success in dealing with false spiritual manifestations. He wrote to his brother Hyrum around this time that he had been "engaged in regulating the churches here as the disciples are numerous and the devil had made many attempts to overthrow them. It has been a serious job but the Lord is with us and we have overcome and have all things regular."[76]

Continuing to Deal with False Spirits: Section 50

Although helpful, Doctrine and Covenants 46 did not do away with false religious enthusiasm completely, and there continued to be disagreement among the Saints. In fact, John Corrill said that unusual behaviors being claimed as legitimate "rose to such a height" that the "elders became so dissatisfied with them that they determined to have something done about it."[77] Parley P. Pratt used strong words to characterize his view of religious enthusiasm when he noted that upon his return from Missouri, these behaviors "grieved the servants of the Lord" and that "many would not turn from their folly, unless God would give a revelation." Continuing to use such characterizations, he suggested that "our weakness and inexperience" could result in errors in "judgment concerning these spiritual phenomena," causing him, John Murdock, and others to go "to Joseph Smith and ask . . . him to inquire of the Lord concerning these spirits or manifestations."[78] John Corrill called the resulting revelation, now recorded in Doctrine and Covenants 50, "very gratifying for it condemned these visionary spirits and gave rules for judging of spirits in general."[79]

As He introduced the revelation, the Lord stated He would address the issue of "the spirits which have gone abroad in the earth" (Doctrine and Covenants 50:1), including "false spirits which have gone forth in the earth, deceiving the world" (verse 2). He further revealed that Satan himself was involved in this attempt to "overthrow you" (verse 3), while characterizing these false spiritual administrations as "abominations in the church that profess my name" (verse 4). He acknowledged the presence of "deceivers and hypocrites" (verse 6) who had "given the adversary power" (verse 7) but who would ultimately be "detected . . . and cut off, either in life or death" (verse 8). He also promised that those influenced would "be reclaimed" (verse 7).

He then engaged the revelatory recipients in a question-and-answer dialogue that began, "Let us reason together . . . as a man reasoneth one with another face to face" (verse 10–11). Referring to prior revelations that indicated they had been ordained to "preach my gospel by the Spirit" (verse 14), He asked if they should feel justified in receiving spirits "they could not understand . . . to be of God" (verse 15) and stated that if both the preacher and the hearer engaged in worship "by the Spirit of truth" (verses 17, 19, and 21), they would "understand one another," and both would be "edified and rejoice together" (verse 22).

The Lord then turned His attention to directing those who preside by referring back to the potential of experiencing spirits "you cannot understand" (verse 31). They were not to "receive . . . that spirit" but rather to "ask of the Father in the name of Jesus; and if he give not unto you that spirit, then you may know that it is not of God" (verse 31). The Lord promised He would provide "power over that spirit" if they would "proclaim against that spirit with a loud voice that it is not of God" (verse 32).

The Lord called three "elders"[80] to "go forth among the churches [branches] and strengthen by the word of exhortation" (verses 37–38), presumably regarding the problem of religious enthusiasm. Parley P. Pratt and John Corrill, who were instigators of the discussions leading to the revelation, were two of the three elders, along with Joseph Wakefield. Edward Partridge apparently had not adequately dealt with the problem in his ecclesiastical position because he was told, "In this thing my servant Edward Partridge is not justified" (verse 39), but he was given a chance to "repent . . . and be forgiven" (verse 39), suggesting he would also bear some responsibility for correcting the problem.

History records that the "elders" did utilize these revelations to regulate the Church in this matter for the next few months. The Prophet himself was also involved when a few weeks later at a conference on the Morley farm, he discerned that the manifestations to Harvey Whitlock and other brethren were of the devil (see Doctrine and Covenants 52, section heading). Likewise, Jared Carter recounted an experience in Amherst, Ohio. He and Sylvester Smith were attending to the sacrament when "a young woman [was] taken with an exercise that brought her on to the floor." They knelt in prayer and "asked our Heavenly Father in the name of Christ that if that spirit that that sister possessed was of him that he would give it to us, but we did not receive that spirit." Acting contrary to the revelation, Sylvester sought to cast out the spirit by laying his hands upon the sister, but it was to no avail. The brothers had a copy of the revelation (that they had apparently made for themselves), and after reviewing it and reading the direction for the elders to "proclaim against the spirit," Jared "then arose and proclaimed against that spirit with a loud voice . . . and from that time forward that spirit never came into the meeting when I was present."[81]

John Whitmer's Response to Being Church Historian and Recorder: Section 47

Doctrine and Covenants 47 is a short and often underemphasized revelation but evidences the faithfulness of John Whitmer in the revelations the Lord gave Joseph Smith. It appoints John to succeed Oliver Cowdery as scribe and recorder together with an additional responsibility.

Following the scribal duties of Martin Harris, Emma Smith, and perhaps even Emma's brother, Reuben Hale,[82] Oliver became the main scribe for the Book of Mormon translation. He also served as scribe for some of Joseph's early revelations and for some of the initial Bible translation. Oliver left for Missouri in October 1830, leaving John to take over temporary responsibility for scribing for the Bible translation. He also participated in compiling and copying revelations. Sidney Rigdon was given Bible scribing duties in December when he visited the Prophet in New York (see Doctrine and Covenants 35:20).

The organization of the Church had dramatically increased the need for various kinds of record keeping. The "Articles and Covenants," section 20, that was revealed before the formal organization of the Church, specified that membership records should be kept. And section 21, which was revealed on April 6, 1830, began with the direction that "there shall be a record kept among you" (Doctrine and Covenants 21:1). Oliver fulfilled the record-keeping responsibility until he left for his mission, then David Whitmer temporarily recorded conference minutes. John agreed to take over for his brother David in recording minutes, but when Joseph said, "You must also keep the Church history," he declined, saying, "I would rather not do it but observed that the will of the Lord be done, and if he desires it, I desire that he would manifest it through Joseph the Seer."[83] The resulting revelation, given "in consequence of not feeling reconciled to write at the request of Joseph without a commandment,"[84] indicated that "it is expedient in me that my servant John should write and keep a regular history, and assist you, my servant Joseph, in transcribing all things which shall be given you, until he is called to further duties. . . . And again, I say unto you that it shall be appointed unto him to keep the church record and history continually; for Oliver Cowdery I have appointed to another office" (Doctrine and Covenants 47:1, 3). Thus, when asked by Joseph to assume this responsibility, John was hesitant, but when Joseph was speaking for the Lord, he accepted.

John was promised in the revelation that "inasmuch as he is faithful," he would be blessed "by the Comforter, to write these things" (Doctrine and Covenants 47:4), and history attests to its fulfillment. After John's appointment, the number of records increased in terms of overall number and size. Greater details accompanied the minutes of Church conferences than had been provided previously, Revelation Book 1 became a treasure trove of Joseph's early revelations, and John wrote a ninety-six-page history that preserved important details relating to the first five years or so of Church history.

The First Manifestation of the Gift of Healing and the Gift to be Healed

The divine privilege of using the priesthood for administering to the sick was revealed as part of the law before the spiritual gifts associated with healing were listed in section 46. "And the elders of the church, two or more, shall be called, and shall pray for and lay their hands upon them in my name; and if they die they shall die unto me, and if they live they shall live unto me" (Doctrine and Covenants 42:44). The first manifestation of these gifts occurred shortly after for the benefit of Alice Johnson, a new convert from Hiram, Ohio.

In February 1831, on a trip to Kirtland, nineteen-year-old Lyman Johnson met Sidney Rigdon, who taught and soon baptized him. Returning home, Lyman announced to his parents, John and Elsa (Alice) Johnson, that he had joined the "Mormonites,"[85] causing them some concern. They counseled with their religious leader, Ezra Booth, who obtained a copy of the Book of Mormon and, accompanied by his wife, Dorcas, took it to the Johnsons' home. As Marinda Johnson later described, the Booths and John and Elsa "sat up all night reading it, and were very much exercised over it."[86] By the following morning, all four of them had experienced the spirit and power of the Book of Mormon. As Ezra later wrote, "The impressions of my mind were deep and powerful, and my feelings were excited to a degree to which I had been a stranger. Like a ghost, it haunted me by night and by day."[87]

Following this experience, the four traveled to meet the Prophet Joseph Smith in Kirtland, along with Symonds and Mehitable Ryder and a Dr. Wright of nearby Wyndham. During a small gathering of members in the Whitney home parlor, the topic of spiritual gifts was discussed, prompting Elsa to ask the Prophet if the power to heal had been restored. She had been afflicted for two years with "chronic rheumatism in the shoulder," and her right arm had been virtually useless.[88] He replied that healing had been restored but waited until the next day for the ideal time and place to lay his hands upon Elsa and pronounce a healing blessing by the authority of the priesthood. Elsa's right arm was instantly restored, as strong and useful as her left.[89] Ironically, the healing of Elsa's arm in March 1831, possibly the first recorded priesthood healing in this dispensation, occurred in the same place where a month earlier, the Lord had revealed His will concerning the restoration of this spiritual gift.

Chapter 6

"Obey the Law Which I Shall Give unto You": Additional Elements of "The Law" and Principles of Church Discipline

Doctrine and Covenants 42

Chronological Summary

- About February 4, 1831—Joseph and Emma Smith arrive in Kirtland and live in the Whitney home
- February 9—Part of "the Law" is revealed (Doctrine and Covenants 42:1–72)
- February 23—The rest of "the Law" is revealed (Doctrine and Covenants 42:73–93)

This is the third chapter that incorporates portions of the revelation known as "the Law" as contained in section 42, the previous chapters having dealt with portions of that section relating to the law of consecration, spiritual gifts, and matters of Church governance. In addition to briefly discussing the opening verses of section 42, this chapter will focus on other elements of the law along with principles of Church discipline.

Chapter 4 introduced the five questions that structured the revelations received as the Lord revealed His law. The first two questions were "Shall the Church come together unto one place or continue in separate establishments?" (answered in verses 1–10) and "[What is] the Law regulating the Church in her present situation till the time of her gathering?" (answered in verses 11–69).

Preach the Gospel and the Commandments

The brethren who gathered together may have been aware of the doctrine of gathering to Zion. In response, the Lord directed all the brethren assembled there to "go forth . . . preaching my gospel, two by two" (Doctrine and Covenants 42:6). He stated that they "shall go forth into the regions westward; and inasmuch as ye shall find them that will receive you ye shall build up my church in every region— Until the time shall come when it shall be revealed unto you . . . [when] the New Jerusalem shall be prepared, that ye may gathered in one" (verses 8–9). Branches were to be established "in every region" (verse 6). Evidence suggests there may have been as many as sixty-one Church branches in the area surrounding Kirtland by the time the Saints left the area in 1838.[90]

Church Discipline

The Lord also added the penalty for disobeying the commandments forbidding stealing, lying, lusting, and committing adultery— being "cast out" (Doctrine and Covenants 42:20, 21, 23, and 24)— and then reiterated the penalty in verse 28, saying, "He that sinneth and repenteth not shall be cast out." Being "cast out" is a reference to excommunication.

This section was not the Prophet's first introduction to Church discipline. The revelation calling for the assembly to receive the law, now found in section 41, expressed the seriousness of the law by indicating, "He that saith he receiveth it and doeth it not, the same is not my disciple, and shall be cast out from among you" (Doctrine and Covenants 41:5). About ten months earlier, the Lord had said that "any member of the church of Christ transgressing, or being overtaken in fault, shall be dealt with as the scriptures direct" (Doctrine and Covenants 20:80). Those directing scriptures probably referred to the Lord directing Alma, who "inquired of me concerning the transgressors" (Mosiah 26:19), that "whosoever will not repent of his sins the same shall not be numbered among my people" (Mosiah 26:32). Alma did as directed, causing those who "would not confess their sins and repent of their iniquity" to no longer be "numbered among the people of the church, and their names were blotted out" (Mosiah 26:36). Likewise, the Lord Himself said that when He came to America following His Resurrection, those who were "unworthy to eat and drink of my flesh and blood . . . shall not be numbered among my people" (3 Nephi 18:29, 31). Moroni said that as a result of this commandment, the leaders of the Church "were strict to observe that there should be no iniquity among them," and "whoso was found to commit iniquity . . . their names were blotted out" (Moroni 6:7). Section 20 likewise indicated, "If any have been expelled from the church . . . their names should be "blotted out of the general church record of names" (verse 83).

Thus, "according to the Articles and Covenants, matters of Church business, including decisions about discipline, were to be made at Church conferences or formal gatherings of elders or members. Participants at these conferences discussed any charges made against Church members, listened to testimonies and confessions, and then made decisions regarding the status of the accused. A variety of cases were settled at early conferences, including instances of domestic abuse, public opposition to the Church, and other misconduct."[91]

Church disciplinary procedures reappear after Doctrine and Covenants 42:69, and most were revealed on February 23, although verses 74–77 were added when the revelation was published in the 1833 Book of Commandments. They first address the sin of adultery, which was an important topic at the time. A noted non–Latter-day Saint of a later generation, Henry Carroll, recorded that the impression of the people in the Kirtland area was that when the Saints on the Morley farm had "all things common," both before and after their conversion, "all things" included "free love."[92] George Albert Smith validates this impression. "Persons came into [the Church] bringing along some of those enthusiasms [wild spiritual manifestations of dubious sources].

Persons who professed to have revelations on every subject and who were read to banish every moral principle under guidance of these false spirits fell into almost any folly, vanity, or excess."[93] It is not surprising, therefore, that the Lord said there were "abominations in the church" perpetrated by "hypocrites . . . who have deceived some . . . but shall be detected and cut off" (Doctrine and Covenants 50:4, 7).

The specific disciplinary procedure to be used stemmed from the principle in the law that "if ye shall find that any persons have left their companions for the sake of adultery, and they themselves are the offenders, and their companions are living, they shall be cast out from among you" (Doctrine and Covenants 42:75). Speaking of adulterers seeking baptism, He said, "Receive none such" (verse 76). If an accusation of adultery arose involving members, the transgressor was to "be tried before two elders of the church, or more, and every word shall be established against him or her by two witnesses of the church. . . . And if it can be, it is necessary that the bishop be present also" (verses 80, 82).

Some transgressions—robbing, stealing, or lying—were to be dealt with by the "law of the land" (verses 84–86), but any manner of iniquity required the transgressor to be "delivered up unto the law, even that of God" (verse 87). Then the Lord outlined varying levels of disciplinary action, confidentiality, and publicity commensurate with whether or not the transgressor offended "many," "openly," or "in secret" (verses 88–92). When an offense occurred, the accused offender and the one offended were to meet "alone" and seek reconciliation. If the offender "confess not," he or she was to be brought before "the church, not to the members, but to the elders. And it shall be done in a meeting, and that not before the world" (verse 89). If found at fault of offending many, the offender's chastisement or rebuke was to occur "before many" (verse 90), and "if any one offend openly, he shall be rebuked openly, that he may be ashamed" (verse 91). Offense "in secret" would be "rebuked in secret, that he may have opportunity to confess in secret . . . that the church may not speak reproachfully of him or her" (verse 92). This was to be a pattern of conducting disciplinary councils in "all things" (verse 93).

Early Church records indicate that the Prophet directed the implementation of these disciplinary instructions. For example, the minutes of the June 1831 conference show "disciplinary" labels after the names of three brethren—"cast off," "cut off," and "cut off rec'd back & re-ordained a Priest." Following his return from Missouri on August 27, 1831, the Prophet discovered that many members of the Church had apostatized,[94] and he would need to direct several localized conferences in September and October to discipline members, train leaders, and conduct other Church business. On October 21, 1831, he met in council with a small group of elders in Hiram, Ohio, to review the case of two young men who were accused of "offering abuse" to Sarah Ann Whitney, Newel K. and Elizabeth Ann Smith Whitney's six-year-old daughter—William Cahoon, the seventeen-year-old son of Reynolds and Thirza Stiles Cahoon, and Peter Devolve, of whom little is known. Despite the young men apparently making confession to Sarah and her family, the Whitneys weren't satisfied, so a council was held to determine whether further action was needed. Without the Whitneys or the young men being present, the elders "voted that this conference send our beloved brethren Joseph Smith Jr. and Sidney Rigdon unto the church in Kirtland to lay before them the decision of this Conference, call before them these two brethren cause them to make sufficient acknowledgement of their sins, or be dealt with according to the law of this Church."[95] William Cahoon went on to be ordained a priest, serve a mission, and participate in Zion's Camp. He was one of the original brethren ordained as Seventies and eventually became a member of the leadership of the Second Quorum of the Seventy. He married Nancy Miranda Gibb and joined with the Saints as they migrated to Missouri, Illinois, and eventually to Utah.

Chapter 7

ADDRESSING "FALSE REPORTS, LIES, AND FOOLISH STORIES": THE SECOND COMING OF JESUS CHRIST

Doctrine and Covenants 45

Chronological Summary

- Early March 1831—Joseph and Emma move to the Morley farm
- About March 7—Joseph receives a revelation in response to "false reports and foolish stories" being published (Doctrine and Covenants 45)
- March 8—The Joseph Smith Translation of the New Testament begins

Widespread Criticism of the Church

Sometime around March 7, 1831,[96] Joseph Smith received a revelation that was titled a "prophecy"[97] and remarked, "At this age of the church many false reports, lies, and fo[o]lish stories were published in the newspapers, and circulated in every direction, to prevent people from investigating the work, or embracing the faith."[98] With the baptism of 127 Saints in the Kirtland area,[99] and that number continually growing to some estimates of over 200 in Kirtland and more than 400 in the larger area,[100] many local newspapers began taking notice and writing about the Church. A number of the articles were derogatory in nature and spread "false reports."

One of the strongest critics of the Church at that time was the editor and founder of the *Painesville Telegraph*, Eber D. Howe. In the issue published on November 16, 1830, Howe included an article titled "The Golden Bible" and popularized the term "Mormonite," becoming one of the first to use this term.[101] During the early days of the Church in Ohio, Howe's sisters, Widow Hutt and Harriet Hutt,[102] joined the Church, and later in 1834 Howe's wife was baptized and became a member of the church that he worked so passionately to discredit.[103] In the *Painesville Telegraph*, Howe and those who wrote for him referred to members of the Church as "fanatics," "a gang of deluded mortals," "deluded beings," "dregs of this community," "profound believers in witchcraft, ghosts, goblins," and "inferior satellites."[104] They also called Joseph Smith's family a "gang of money diggers" and referred to the witnesses of the Book of Mormon as "pious reprobates."[105] Later in 1831 the *Telegraph* stated that Joseph's revelations were "volumes of . . . trash."[106] A misleading article in the *Telegraph* led Joseph Smith to include the following in the history of the Church: "A great earth-quake in China, which destroyed from one to two hundred thousand inhabitants, was burlesqued in some papers, as 'Mormonism in China.'"[107] Howe's articles were circulated and reprinted in many newspapers throughout the country, adding to Joseph's statement that many false stories were being "published in the newspapers, and circulated in every direction."[108] In 1834 Howe published *Mormonism Unvailed* [sic], one of the first anti–Latter-day Saint books.

Another critic of the Church who was actively publishing disparaging articles in the spring of 1831 was Alexander Campbell. This was especially damaging in that many of the new converts of the budding Church in Ohio came from congregations that were originally formed as part of the Campbellite movement. Two of the Campbells' in-laws were among the earliest converts to the church, Julia and John Murdock.[109]

In addition to his Reformed Baptist movement, Campbell's influence was strongly felt due to the two newspapers he founded, the *Christian Baptist* and the *Millennial Harbinger*. The *Millennial Harbinger* first appeared on January 4, 1830, with the following objective: "Devoted to the destruction of sectarianism, infidelity, and anti-Christian doctrine and practice. It shall have for its object the development and introduction of that political and religious order of society called The Millennium, which will be the consummation of that ultimate amelioration of society proposed in the Christian Scriptures."[110] On February 5, 1831, Campbell published an article in the *Millennial Harbinger* just months after the baptism of Sidney Rigdon and Parley P. Pratt, both of whom were preachers and leaders in the Campbellite movement in northeast Ohio. It was titled "Delusions" and attacked the authenticity of the Book of Mormon by stating that "every age of the world has produced impostors and delusions" and that the Book of Mormon was only "the most recent and the most impudent delusion which has appeared in our time."[111] This article was distributed throughout the country in various newspapers and became an early anti–Latter-day Saint tract.

The Lord's Response

Articles written and distributed by Eber D. Howe, Alexander Campbell, and others led to Joseph's observation that many false and foolish reports were being circulated in papers, prompting him to petition the Lord on the matter. Introducing the Lord's reply, he wrote, "But to the joy of the Saints who had to struggle against every thing that prejudice and wickedness could invent, I received the following."[112] This "prophecy" would later be known as section 45 of the Doctrine and Covenants.

Among other hopeful and inspiring doctrines, this prophecy addressed topics that would have been empowering given all of the persecution suffered by the Saints—topics such as the New Jerusalem, Zion, the gathering to safety, and the Second Coming of Jesus Christ. Through the translation of the Book of Mormon, and as Joseph continued to translate the Bible, he and the Saints had learned and would learn more about the city of Zion, the people of Enoch, and the ushering in of the Second Coming of Jesus Christ and His kingdom.

Revelations Leading Up to Section 45

Regarding Zion and the New Jerusalem, the Book of Mormon taught, "This people will I establish in this land, unto the fulfilling of the covenant which I made with your father Jacob; and it shall be a New Jerusalem. And the powers of heaven shall be in the midst of this people; yea, even I will be in the midst of you" (3 Nephi 20:22). The Lord later revealed that with the coming forth of the Book of Mormon, the Lord would gather together Israel and "establish again among them Zion" (Doctrine and Covenants 29:1). He further declared that the house of Israel shall come together and build a city, which shall be called the New Jerusalem. . . . And then shall the power of heaven come down among them; and I also will be in the midst" (3 Nephi 21:23, 25). In the book of Ether, the Saints learned that the Americas were "a choice land above all other lands, a chosen land of the Lord . . . and that it was a place of the New Jerusalem, which should come down out of heaven . . . and that a New Jerusalem should be built up upon this land" (Ether 13:2–3, 6). This understanding of New Jerusalem being built in the Americas became a driving force for the Saints, and they began to look forward to the day of its fulfillment.

Even before the Church was officially established, Joseph received revelations instructing him and others to "seek to bring forth and establish the cause of Zion" (Doctrine and Covenants 6:6; 11:6; 12:6), a term used by many Christians to denote the spreading of the gospel. In September 1830 Oliver Cowdery received a mission call to "go unto the Lamanites and preach my gospel" (Doctrine and Covenants 28:8). In that same revelation, Oliver was corrected by the Lord for being deceived by Hiram Page's claims of receiving revelation concerning the building of Zion. The Lord said, "No man knoweth where the city Zion shall be built, but it shall be given hereafter. Behold, I say unto you that it shall be on the borders by the Lamanites" (Doctrine and Covenants 28:9), referring to western Missouri and the unincorporated Indian Territory west of it. Although the mission call was to preach among the Lamanites, the Lord would use this mission as an important step to help Joseph Smith discover the location of the city of New Jerusalem. The Lord revealed that Peter Whitmer Jr. (see Doctrine and Covenants 30:5–6), Parley P. Pratt (see Doctrine and Covenants

32:2), and Ziba Petersen (see Doctrine and Covenants 32:3) should join Oliver on his mission to the "borders by the Lamanites." Later in September the Lord revealed that He would "gather mine elect" and that "they shall be gathered in unto one place upon this land" (Doctrine and Covenants 29:7, 8).

With the assistance of Oliver Cowdery as scribe, Joseph had begun the work of translating the Bible in June 1830.[113] When Oliver left for his mission, others worked as scribes in the translation process— John Whitmer, then Emma Smith, and eventually Sidney Rigdon.[114] In November and December 1830 Joseph dictated passages about the patriarch Enoch and the formation of the city of Zion. He learned that Enoch was called of the Lord to "go forth" amongst the people and "open [his] mouth" (Moses 6:32). Through his efforts, Enoch established a people the Lord called Zion "because they were of one heart and one mind, and dwelt in righteousness; and there was no poor among them" (Moses 7:18). Joseph also learned that Enoch established a "City of Holiness, even Zion" and that "Zion, in the process of time, was taken up into heaven" (Moses 7:19, 21). In that same revelation, Joseph was instructed that prior to His Second Coming, the Lord would "gather out mine elect from the four quarters of the earth, unto a place which I shall prepare, an Holy City, that my people may gird up their loins, and be looking forth for the time of my coming . . . and it shall be called Zion, a New Jerusalem" (Moses 7:62). Enoch's City of Zion would descend from heaven and together with the New Jerusalem would be received into the bosom of God. "They shall see us; and we will fall upon their necks, and they shall fall upon our necks, and we will kiss each other; And there shall be mine abode, and it shall be Zion" (Moses 7:63–64). In March 1831 the Lord instructed Joseph about His Second Coming and referenced Enoch and his city as a symbol of the glorious day of his return (see Doctrine and Covenants 45:11–12). With these beautiful promises, it is no wonder that Joseph and the Saints sought so diligently to establish the cause of Zion and bring about the establishment of a "City of Holiness, even Zion."

On February 9, 1831, shortly after Joseph Smith's arrival to Kirtland, the Lord instructed the Saints about what they needed to do while waiting for further revelation about Zion.[115] They were instructed to continue to "build up my church in every region—Until the time shall come when it shall be revealed unto you from on high, when the city of New Jerusalem shall be prepared, that ye may be gathered in one, that ye may be my people and I will be your God" (Doctrine and Covenants 42:8–9). Joseph was also told, "Thou shalt ask, and it shall be revealed unto you in mine own due time where the New Jerusalem shall be built" (Doctrine and Covenants 42:62).

Around March 7, 1831, Joseph received further clarification on the establishment of Zion. Against the backdrop of the Second Coming, the Lord instructed Joseph, "Ye hear of wars in foreign lands, but behold, I say unto you, they are nigh, even at your doors" (Doctrine and Covenants 45:63). In helping the Saints better understand the need to move from their homes in New York and Pennsylvania, and prepare them for future moves and sacrifices, the Lord taught:

> Wherefore I, the Lord, have said, gather ye out from the eastern lands, assemble ye yourselves together ye elders of my church. . . .
>
> And with one heart and with one mind, gather up your riches that ye may purchase an inheritance which shall hereafter be appointed unto you.
>
> And it shall be called the New Jerusalem, a land of peace, a city of refuge, a place of safety for the Saints of the Most High God;
>
> And the glory of the Lord shall be there, and the terror of the Lord also shall be there, insomuch that the wicked will not come unto it, and it shall be called Zion. (Doctrine and Covenants 45:64–67)

The Lord further instructed that "people must flee unto Zion for safety" and that Zion will "be the only people that shall not be at war one with another" (verses 68–69), along with the beautiful promise that "it shall come to pass that the righteous shall be gathered out from among all nations, and shall come to Zion, singing with songs of everlasting joy" (verse 71). It is easy to see why Joseph stated that this revelation was a "joy of the Saints."[116]

Eventually, on June 6, 1831, Joseph received a revelation instructing him and many other elders to travel to Missouri, which the Lord said was "the land which I will consecrate unto my people" (Doctrine and Covenants 52:2), saying that the faithful the Saints should "rejoice upon the land of Missouri, which is the land of your inheritance"

(Doctrine and Covenants 52:42). Joseph left Kirtland, Ohio, on June 19 and arrived in Independence, Jackson County, Missouri, on July 14.[117] After arriving, Joseph began ruminating on the question of Zion: "When will the wilderness blossom as the rose; when will Zion be built up in her glory, and where will thy Temple stand unto which all nations shall come in the last days?"[118] On July 20 he was taught, "Missouri . . . is the land which I have appointed and consecrated for the gathering of the Saints. Wherefore, this is the land of promise, and the place for the city of Zion. . . . Behold, the place which is now called Independence is the center place" (Doctrine and Covenants 57:1–3). Joseph and the Saints now knew that the City of Holiness, even Zion, was to be built in Independence, Jackson County, Missouri.

Joseph Smith Translation of the Bible: A Switch from the Old Testament to the New Testament

In Doctrine and Covenants 45, the Lord also instructed Joseph concerning his efforts in translating the Bible. Beginning in June 1830, Joseph and his scribes primarily focused on translating the Old Testament, beginning with the book of Genesis and the visions of Moses. By March 1831 Joseph and his scribes had created a sixty-one-page manuscript account of the visions of Moses and a revised version of the Old Testament book of Genesis, chapters 1–24 and 41.[119] Section 45 instructed him to translate the New Testament so "that ye may be prepared for the things to come" (Doctrine and Covenants 45:61). On March 8, 1831, Joseph Smith and Sidney Rigdon began translating the New Testament in a document titled "A Translation of the New Testament translated by the power of God." They began with Matthew 1:1 and translated sixty-five pages through Matthew 26:71 before the translation was interrupted by Joseph and Sidney's travels to Missouri in June 1831.[120]

Chapter 8

"True and Faithful": Personal Revelations to John Whitmer

Doctrine and Covenants 47

On March 8, 1831, the Lord directed John Whitmer to "serve as the Church historian and recorder, replacing Oliver Cowdery" (Doctrine and Covenants 47, section heading). Before this revelation, the Prophet had invited John to fill this position, to which John replied, "I would rather not do it but observed that the will of the Lord be done, and if he desires it, I desire that he would manifest it through Joseph the Seer" (Doctrine and Covenants 47, section heading). In response to Joseph's petition, the Lord referred to John as "my servant" and directed that John "should write and keep a regular history" (verse 1) and "keep the church record" (verse 3). "After Joseph received this revelation, John accepted and served in his appointed office" (Doctrine and Covenants 47, section heading) because he believed he had been "commanded of the Lord and Savior Jesus Christ."[121] His formal appointment came a month later on April 9, 1831, when he was assigned "to keep the Church record & history by the voice of ten Elders," a wise decision in light of the fact that probably "few were as well positioned to observe and record the important events of the church."[122]

John considered that his responsibility was to pick up where Oliver Cowdery left off. His records include his intention to "proceed to continue this record"[123] and then later noted, "Oliver Cowdery has written the commencement of the church history commencing at the time of the finding of the plates, up to June 12, 1831. From this date I have written the things that I have written."[124]

John had evidenced being "true and faithful" prior to this appointment. He supported the Prophet when he resided with the Whitmer family in Fayette, New York, including serving as a scribe for a portion of the Book of Mormon translation. He was one of the Eight Witnesses to the Book of Mormon and helped Joseph arrange and copy his revelations in July 1830. A revelation given in June 1829, the first of five revelations directed to him, began with the words "Hearken, my servant John, and listen to the words of Jesus Christ, your Lord and your Redeemer" (Doctrine and Covenants 15:1). He was later directed to study and preach in June 1830, in the same revelation in which the law of common consent was revealed (Doctrine and Covenants 26). Three months later, similar divine direction was given to him in the revelation now known as Doctrine and Covenants 30. The 1831 commandments recorded in sections 47 and 69 were the fourth and fifth revelations directed to him. His faithfulness was further demonstrated when he was sent to Kirtland, a month before Joseph arrived, to deal with the problems stemming from a lack of trained priesthood leadership.

Learning to serve as a historian was a lengthy process and required ongoing encouragement from the Prophet and others. As shown, section 69 was the second commandment John had received regarding his responsibility. About a year later, the Prophet wrote in a letter to John, "I exhort Bro John also to remember the commandment to him to keep a history of the church & the gathering and be sure to shew himself approved whereunto he hath been called." In a July 1833 letter, John asked Oliver to request further instructions, to which a response was received the following January. In John's patriarchal blessing, given by the Prophet himself in September 1835, part of the blessing concerned the history he was writing, promising that he "shall make a choice record of Israel."[125]

Chapter 9

"I Will Pour Out My Spirit upon Them in the Day That They Assemble Themselves Together": June Conference

Doctrine and Covenants 52

Chronological Summary

- Late February 1831—The Saints are instructed to prepare for a conference (Doctrine and Covenants 44)
- June 3–6—The June conference is held (Doctrine and Covenants 52)

In the latter part of February, the Lord provided a revelation that comprises the last of the four sections given during the six weeks Joseph and Emma Smith lived with the Whitneys. He directed "that the elders of my church should be called together" for a conference—a gathering for holders of the priesthood from their various missions and also for the general Church membership—and promised that if they were "faithful, and exercise faith in me, I will pour out my Spirit upon

69

them in the day that they assemble themselves together" (Doctrine and Covenants 44:1–2). In the Articles and Covenants, now known as section 20 of the Doctrine and Covenants, the Lord had said, "The several elders composing this Church of Christ are to meet in conference once in three months to [do] Church business whatsoever is necessary."[126] In compliance with that command, conferences were held June 6, 1830, where the "Articles and Covenants" were approved by common consent; September 25, 1830, around which time six revelations were received, constituting four sections of the Doctrine and Covenants (28, 29, 30, and 31); and January 2, 1831, which had the express purpose of strengthening the branches and building the Saints' faith sufficient to heed the command to gather to "the Ohio" (Doctrine and Covenants 38:32). At that time, conferences were primarily councils designed to do what the revelation said—conduct "Church business"—but like today, they were also revelatory events and included preaching, ordaining, disciplinary action, and training.

Conference Preparations and Initial Session

In April, early June was set as the time for the conference, the first to be held in Ohio, and letters and verbal notices "called together . . . the elders of my church." It was to be a four-day event—Friday, June 3, was to be a preparatory day, and the agenda for the conference was set by revelation;[127] Saturday, June 4, saw the Prophet introduce the "high priesthood"; Sunday, June 5, was a meeting for the general membership; and Monday, June 6, involved issuing mission calls following the commands in the revelation now known as section 52.

Following the conference, the elders were to return to the mission field "into the regions round about," empowered to "preach repentance unto the people" (Doctrine and Covenants 44:3). The Lord promised, "Many shall be converted, insomuch that ye shall obtain power to organize yourselves" (Doctrine and Covenants 44:4). He had made a similar promise to the New York Saints, stating they would "be endowed with power from on high" (Doctrine and Covenants 38:32) if they moved to Ohio, and the histories of those who attended the conference indicate that they believed this promise was fulfilled in part at the June conference. "The power to organize" led to the organization of sixty-one branches in Ohio over time. According to Ezra Booth, it was widely held "that the work of miracles would commence at the ensuing conference."[128]

The preliminary meeting's revelatory directions included that "such of the elders as were considered worthy, should be ordained to the high priesthood"[129] (office of high priest) on Saturday, June 4. It was also revealed that at the time of the ordinations, false spiritual gifts would be manifest as "the man of sin should be revealed,"[130] and contrastingly, the Prophet also made it known that some should see "their Savior, face to face."[131]

Second Session

Because most of the New York Saints who had intended to migrate to Ohio arrived during May, nearly all Church members—numbering over 600—were living in Ohio settlements in or around Kirtland. Sixty-two of those members who held the priesthood—43 elders and 19 priests and teachers—gathered in the schoolhouse on the Morley farm for the second conference session. This fourteen-square-foot log structure was designed to hold less than twenty-five school children seated on rough-hewn benches, so the sixty-two men filled the benches, sat on windowsills, or sat outside near the open doors and windows. (A larger number that included women and children attended on Sunday, June 5, to hear the preaching of sermons.)

The conference session commenced with prayer and a long "exhortation" by the Prophet, and several brethren later wrote of its effect upon them. Jared Carter wrote that "not withstanding he is not naturally talented for a speaker yet he was filled with the power of the Holy Ghost so that he spoke as I never heard man speak for God by the power of the Holy Ghost spoke in him."[132] Parley P. Pratt said that Joseph "spake in great power, as he was moved by the Holy Ghost; and the spirit of power and of testimony rested down upon the Elders in a marvelous manner."[133] Levi Hancock recalled that Joseph taught "the kingdom that Christ spoke of that was like a grain of mustard seed was now before him and some should see it put forth its branches and the angels of heaven would someday come like birds to its branches just as the Savior said and some of you shall live to see it come with great glory some of you must die for the testimony of this work."[134] John Whitmer added that "the Spirit of the Lord fell upon Joseph in an unusual manner" and that Joseph prophesied "that John the Revelator was then among the ten tribes of Israel . . . to prepare them for their return" and "many more things that I have not written."[135]

Joseph's exhortation was followed by exhortation and prayer by Sidney Rigdon, and then all the elders present were invited to make exhortations. The term "exhortation" probably means being left to speak as moved upon by the Spirit, so there could have been the bearing of testimony, doctrinal exposition, expounding of scripture, or actual exhortation and preaching. The minutes of the conference then record that Joseph ordained five brethren to the "high priesthood"; shortly thereafter, Lyman Wight ordained eighteen more, including Joseph himself; and then Bishop Edward Partridge "blessed those who were ordained in the name of Christ according to commandment."[136] The term "high priesthood" had reference at the time to the office of high priest, and conference participants associated it with receiving additional power.[137] Later, "high priesthood" became a term distinct from "high priest" and referred to the Melchizedek Priesthood (see Doctrine and Covenants 107:9). Parley P. Pratt explained how the brethren eventually came to understand the differences between the offices of elder and high priest and between offices of the priesthood and the priesthood itself: "Several [brethren] were then selected by revelation, through President Smith, and ordained to the High Priesthood after the order of the Son of God; which is after the order of Melchisedec. This was the first occasion in which this priesthood had been revealed and conferred upon the Elders in this dispensation, although the office of an Elder is the same in a certain degree, but not in the fulness. On this occasion I was ordained to this holy ordinance and calling by President Smith."[138]

Joseph's first experience with these terms probably occurred with the Book of Mormon translation. For example, in Alma 13, Alma described righteous men being "called by this holy calling, and ordained unto the high priesthood of the holy order of God . . . this high priesthood being after the order of his Son . . . being called with a holy calling, and ordained with a holy ordinance, and taking upon them the high priesthood of the holy order, which calling, and ordinance, and high priesthood, is without beginning or end" (Alma 13:6–8). Similarly, in June 1830 similar words were revealed to Joseph that were related to Genesis 14: "Now Melchizedek was a man of faith, who wrought righteousness; and when a child he feared God, and stopped the mouths of lions, and quenched the violence of fire. And thus, having been approved of God, he was ordained an high priest after the order of the covenant which God made with Enoch, It being after the order of the Son of God" (Joseph Smith Translation, Genesis 14:25–27 [in Genesis 14:24, footnote *a*]).

Prior to the ordinations, the Prophet had addressed Lyman Wight, saying, "You shall see the Lord and meet him near the corner of the house." After his ordination, Lyman "stepped out on the floor and said, 'I now see God and Jesus Christ at his right hand let them kill me I should not feel death as I am now.'" Joseph likewise testified, "I now see God, and Jesus Christ at his right hand, let them kill me, I should not feel death as I am now."[139] John Whitmer added that Joseph "saw the heavens opened, and the Son of man sitting on the right hand of the Father. Making intercession for his brethren, the Saints. He said that God would work a work in these last days that tongue cannot express, and the mind is not capable to conceive. The glory of the Lord shone around."[140]

Other miraculous events accompanied the priesthood ordinations. Lyman Wight testified of "the visible manifestations of the power of God as plain as could have been on the day of Pentecost," including "the healing of the sick, casting out devils, speaking in unknown tongues, discerning of spirits, and prophesying with mighty power."[141] In fulfillment of Friday's prophecy that the man of sin would be revealed, Harvey Whitlock was seized by a power following his ordination that caused bodily contortions and restricted his speech—common behaviors exhibited by the Saints who were engaging in false, ecstatic experiences. He literally turned black, his fingers were set like claws, and his eyes were shaped like an owl's eyes—"a frightful object to the view of the beholder."[142] Joseph invited Harvey to speak, perhaps to test the source of the influences on him, but Harvey could only reply with signs. Hyrum Smith, Joseph's brother, expressed uneasiness: "Joseph, that is not of God."[143] After some discussion based on the principles of discernment given in section 50, Joseph rebuked the devil and cast him out. In that revelation, the Lord had said, "If you behold a spirit manifested that you cannot understand, and you receive not that spirit, ye shall ask of the Father in the name of Jesus; and if he give not unto you that spirit, then you may know that it is not of God. And it shall be given unto you, power over that spirit; and you shall proclaim against that spirit with a loud voice that it is not of God" (Doctrine and Covenants 50:31–32).

While the brethren were dealing with Levi's experience, ecstatic expressions broke out amongst several brethren. Leman Copley, a 214-pound former Shaker accustomed to such expressions, "turned a complete summerset in the house and came his back across a bench and lay helpless."[144] Joseph instructed Lyman to cast Satan out of Leman, which he did, but Satan "immediately entered another." Harvey Green fell "bound and screamed like a panther."[145] The record makes it clear that these expressions that were now clearly esteemed as demonic continued all day and well into the night, causing the leading brethren to deal with each on a one-on-one basis. It was understood that these experiences occurred "for the express purpose that the Elders should become acquainted with the devices of Satan; and after that they would possess knowledge sufficient to manage him."[146] Therefore, ecstatic expressions pretty much came to end, while other legitimate spiritual gifts were manifest widely.

Third and Fourth Sessions

On Sunday, June 5, families attended the next session with the priesthood brethren. Although the exact number is unknown, over 200 Saints had moved from New York, and the Morley farm was full of families. Levi Hancock said the Saints gathered "on the hill in a field where there was a large concourse of people collected."[147] Interestingly, one woman traveling alone fell from the wagon she was driving and "to every appearance was mortally bruised and she was not expected to live." But Simeon Carter "took her by the hand and said I command you in the name of Jesus Christ to rise up and walk and she arose and walked from room to room."[148] A number of long sermons were preached, including one by the Prophet during which he said, "From that time the Elders would have large congregations to speak to and they must soon take their departure into the regions west."[149]

Later that night the Prophet received a revelation that came "by an heavenly vision."[150] The next day, the final day of the conference, he presented the revelation to the brethren assembled, calling many of them to travel as missionaries to western Missouri to hold a conference at which the Lord would reveal "the land of your inheritance" (Doctrine and Covenants 52:5), or in other words, the land of Zion, the New Jerusalem.

Chapter 10

"This Is the Land of Promise and the Place for the City of Zion": Zion in Missouri

Doctrine and Covenants 52, 57–62

Chronological Summary

- June 19, 1831—Joseph Smith and a company of others leave for Missouri
- July 14—Joseph Smith and his company arrive in Jackson County, Missouri
- July 17—An unpublished revelation is received
- July 20—The location of Zion (the New Jerusalem) is revealed (Doctrine and Covenants 57)
- August 1—The Lord reveals various divine instructions for Zion (Doctrine and Covenants 58)
- August 2—The land of Zion is consecrated and dedicated
- August 3—The Independence, Missouri, temple site is dedicated

- August 7—The Prophet receives instruction about the Sabbath (Doctrine and Covenants 59)
- August 8—The Prophet receives instruction about returning to Ohio (Doctrine and Covenants 60)
- August 12—Contentions arise at McIlwaine's Bend on the Missouri River (Doctrine and Covenants 61)
- August 13—An unexpected missionary reunion occurs on the return trip (Doctrine and Covenants 62)
- August 27—Joseph Smith and his company arrive in Kirtland

The Prophet Joseph Smith taught that Zion "was the most important temporal object in view,"[151] stating that "the building up of Zion is a cause that has interested the people of God in every age; . . . they have looked forward with joyful anticipation to the day in which we live; and fired with heavenly and joyful anticipations they have sung and written and prophesied of this our day."[152] By the time the Lord specifically directed the building up of Zion in Missouri, Joseph had been well prepared to understand the deeper meanings behind the truth that "Zion (the New Jerusalem) will be built upon the American continent" (Articles of Faith 1:10). That preparation began with the Book of Mormon translation, then continued with the Bible translation and direct revelations that preceded the revelation now found in section 52.

The word *Zion* appears in the Book of Mormon twenty-seven times, mostly in quotes of Isaiah from the brass plates. Disregarding any possible mention of it in the lost 116 pages, and recognizing that the small plates of Nephi were probably translated after Mormon's abridgement of the large plates, Joseph would have first seen the word *Zion* in Mosiah 12:21—"How beautiful upon the mountains are the feet of him . . . that saith unto Zion, Thy God reigneth." From these verses, Joseph would have seen that "the Lord shall bring again Zion" (3 Nephi 16:18) and that, indeed, He would "gather in, from their long dispersion, my people, O house of Israel, and shall establish again among them my Zion" (3 Nephi 21:1). Likewise, he may have connected these preparatory verses to those that state that America "was the place of the New Jerusalem" (Ether 13:3), that it would be "built up upon this land" (Ether 13:6), and that it also "should come down out of heaven and [be the place of] the holy sanctuary of the Lord" (Ether 13:3).

The first reference to Zion in the Prophet's revelations appears in the revelation directed to Oliver Cowdery now found in Doctrine and Covenants 6: "establish the cause of Zion" (verse 6). It is first referred to as a specific place when the Lord instructed the Lamanite missionaries to leave on their mission to the same place the "city Zion shall be built . . . on the borders by the Lamanites" (Doctrine and Covenants 28:9, referring to the Missouri-Kansas Territory border). When preparing to leave on that mission, Oliver Cowdery's written covenant that he and his companions signed promised "to rear up a pillar as a witness where the Temple of God shall be built, in the glorious New-Jerusalem."[153] Following their three-week preaching in Kirtland in late October and November 1830, the missionaries arrived in their appointed destination, the area that would come to be known as Zion in late January 1831. It is discussed in relation to the gathering of Israel and the Second Coming of Christ in sections 45 and 49, and in the former the Lord said that Zion "shall be called the New Jerusalem" (Doctrine and Covenants 45:66). Around the time Joseph was translating or receiving a portion of the book of Enoch that appears in the book of Moses—wherein "Zion" is mentioned eighteen times and "New Jerusalem" once—the Lord referred to Himself as "the same which have taken the Zion of Enoch into mine own bosom" (Doctrine and Covenants 38:4) in one of the three sections commanding the New York Saints to "go to the Ohio" (Doctrine and Covenants 38).

Another term that had been used by the Lord in section 38 that had reference to Zion was "the land of your inheritance" (verse 19). On the night of the third day of the June 1831 conference that was held on the Morley farm, the Lord directed that the next conference "shall be held in Missouri, upon the land which I will consecrate unto my people, which are a remnant of Jacob and those who are heirs according to the covenant" (Doctrine and Covenants 52:2). While they were there, it was to "be made known . . . the land of your inheritance" (verse 5), meaning the land of Zion. When the revelation was read at the conference the next day, it directed that Joseph, Sidney Rigdon, Martin Harris, and Edward Partridge "leave their homes, and journey to the land of Missouri" (verses 3, 24, 41). Twenty-four other brethren were directed to "take their journey also, preaching the word by the way unto this same land" (verse 22). They were all promised, "If ye are faithful ye shall assemble yourselves together to rejoice upon the land of Missouri, which is the land of your inheritance, which is now the land of your enemies. But, behold, I, the Lord, will hasten the city in its time" (verses 42–43).

After the June Conference: Sections 53–56

Four revelations given on the Morley farm right after the conference dealt directly with Zion. The revelation that now appears in section 53 addressed Algernon Sidney Gilbert, appointing him "to be an agent unto this church in the place which shall be appointed by the bishop" (verse 4), which turned out to be in Missouri. Following the failure of Leman Copley to honor his covenant to consecrate his farm in Thompson, the Colesville Saints were instructed to "flee the land" and "take your journey into the regions westward, unto the land of Missouri, unto the borders of the Lamanites" (Doctrine and Covenants 54:7, 8).

In June 1831 William and Sally Phelps brought their family from New York to meet the Prophet prior to their baptism. When Joseph sought the Lord on their behalf, the Lord said He had already "called and chosen" William to "do the work of printing," telling him that after he would be baptized, he was to "take [his] journey" with Joseph and Sidney to the "land of [his] inheritance" in Missouri (Doctrine and Covenants 55:1, 4, 5). Joseph Coe, a recent convert from New York, was also directed to "take his journey with them" (verse 6). On June 15 the Lord revoked Ezra Thayre's mission call; directed his companion, Thomas B. Marsh, to travel to Missouri with Selah J. Griffin, Newel Knight's companion; and told Newel to continue as the Colesville branch president, leading the Colesville Saints to Missouri (see Doctrine and Covenants 56).

In Missouri

Joseph Smith, Sidney Rigdon, Martin Harris, Edward Partridge, William W. Phelps, Joseph Coe, and Sidney and Elizabeth Gilbert left for Missouri on June 19, 1831. They traveled south to Cincinnati by utilizing the Ohio-Erie Canal, then booked passage on a steamboat that headed down the Ohio River then up the Mississippi to St. Louis. Meanwhile, the Colesville Saints departed Thompson, Ohio, in twenty-four wagons and traveled to Wellsville, Ohio. There they left the wagons and also traveled by steamboat to St. Louis where they met the Prophet's company.

At St. Louis, Sidney and the Gilberts waited several days before continuing on by river with the Colesville Saints while the other members of Joseph's group traveled by foot. They arrived in Independence, Jackson County, Missouri, on July 14, and the Colesville group arrived the following week. They were met by Oliver Cowdery, Peter Whitmer Jr., and Ziba Peterson, three of the four original Lamanite missionaries, as well as Frederick G. Williams who had joined the missionaries in Kirtland.[154] Joseph described the journey as "long and tedious" and said they arrived only after "suffering many privations and hardships."[155] Newel Knight said the task of leading the Colesville Saints "required all the wisdom"[156] he possessed.

Almost all of the missionaries called in Doctrine and Covenants 52 were ready to leave Kirtland within two weeks of their call. Because they had been commanded to "not build upon another's foundation, neither journey in another's track" (Doctrine and Covenants 52:33), each companionship chose to travel a different route. Some of the missionaries were more successful than others as they "preach[ed] by the way" (Doctrine and Covenants 52:23), and some were "exceedingly blessed even above measure" (Doctrine and Covenants 58:61). Parley P. and Orson Pratt "suffered the hardships incident to a new and, in many places, unsettled country,"[157] but they baptized many people and organized branches in the states they passed through, not arriving in Jackson County until September. Zebedee Coltrin and Levi Hancock also enjoyed success, baptizing "upwards of one hundred souls."[158] After leaving Kirtland, they headed south, and when they reached Winchester, Indiana, they "continued to preach . . . in the regions round about until we had raised a large branch of the Church. . . . In a short time we had about one hundred members."[159] In Ward Township, Indiana, Levi used the fact that his father had fought in the Revolutionary War, and that his relative John Hancock was the first signer of the Declaration of Independence, to soften the hearts of his listeners, some of whom were conspiring to do him and Zebedee harm. He recalled, "After the meeting we went to the water and baptized seventeen out of that crowd who the day before were going to mob us."[160] As a result, Zebedee didn't arrive in Jackson County until October, and illness delayed Levi until November. (While in Missouri, Levi built the building that housed the printing press and the Phelps family.) Other missionaries traveled more quickly. Lyman Wight and John Corrill, for example, left Kirtland on June 14 and arrived on August 13.

The Land of Zion: Section 57

While in Missouri, Joseph received six revelations, recorded in Doctrine and Covenants 57–62, and conducted a number of divinely directed matters of business. He also received another revelation prior to section 57 that was unpublished. Although these seven revelations were not received on the Morley farm, they were received during the time the Prophet and Emma's "official" residence was the small frame house on that farm. These seven revelations also provide context for subsequent revelations received on the Morley farm when Joseph returned to Kirtland and are a critical part of the Restoration that characterized the overall Kirtland period of Church history.

The revelation now known as Doctrine and Covenants 57 was given in response to the Prophet's inquiry: "When will the wilderness blossom as the rose? When will Zion be built up in her glory, and where will Thy temple stand, unto which all nations shall come in the last days?"[161] Such an inquiry would naturally result from the Lord's promise in section 52 to make "known . . . the land of your inheritance" (verse 5), but Joseph's desire for light and knowledge stemmed from deeper concerns than those suggested by a surface interpretation of his request. His history records that he spent considerable time pondering on the condition of the American Indians living west of the Missouri River. Also, when the missionaries arrived, they were met with disappointment. Rather than the lush forests of Ohio, they encountered a somewhat desolate environment by comparison—scattered trees, brush, and open prairie. Independence was a frontier town used as a staging location for immigrants traveling west on the Santa Fe Trail, so there wasn't much to it. Also, every sort of person and culture were present, including those of questionable morals who exhibited a lifestyle far from the ideals of Zion. Ezra Boothe depicted it as "a new Town, containing a courthouse, built of brick, two or three merchant stores, and fifteen or twenty dwelling houses, built mostly of logs hewed on both sides."[162] Missionary efforts also yielded fewer converts than expected, and the initial four missionaries who had preceded them had been denied access to the Lamanites they were commissioned to teach.

The Prophet recorded elsewhere that he "view[ed] the country" before "seeking diligently at the hand of God," whereupon the Lord "manifested himself unto me, and designated to me and others, the very spot upon which he designed to commence the work of the gathering, and the upbuilding of an holy city, which should be called Zion."[163] This manifestation comprises Doctrine and Covenants 57, wherein the Lord announced that the land they had gathered to was "the land which I have appointed and consecrated for the gathering of the saints . . . the land of promise, and the place for the city of Zion" (verses 1–2).[164] The Lord also identified Independence as the "center place" and a lot that was "lying westward . . . not far from the courthouse" as a "spot for the temple" (verse 3). The temple lot was to be "purchased by the Saints" along with "every tract lying westward, even unto the line running directly between Jew and Gentile; And also every tract bordering by the prairies" (verses 4–5).[165]

Four brethren received verification and some explanation regarding their previously revealed assignments to "be planted" (Doctrine and Covenants 57:11) in Zion. Sidney Gilbert was to "receive moneys, to be an agent unto the church, to buy land" (verse 6), and to "establish a store, that he may sell goods without fraud, that he may obtain money to buy lands" in order to "obtain whatsoever things the disciples may need to plant them in their inheritance" (verse 8). Edward Partridge was to "divide unto the Saints their inheritance" with the help of his counselors—"those whom he has appointed to assist him" (verse 7)—John Corrill and Isaac Morley. These four brethren were to "make preparations for those families which have been commanded to come to this land . . . and plant them in their inheritance" (verse 15), which would have included the Colesville Saints. William W. Phelps was again directed to "be established as a printer unto the church" (verse 11), and Oliver Cowdery was commanded to "assist him" (verse 13).

On Sunday, July 13, a worship service was held and two converts were baptized. The sixty Colesville Saints arrived the following Tuesday.

Further Instructions for Zion: Section 58

After the July 20 revelation, Joseph and Edward Partridge contended about the land that was to be purchased for the Saints. Edward argued that other parcels of land of higher quality should be purchased instead of the ones designated by Joseph.[166] These circumstances prompted Joseph to seek additional guidance, which came on August 1 in the revelation now recorded as Doctrine and Covenants 58. The visionary encouragement in the first few verses—"Ye cannot behold with your natural eyes, for the present time, the design of your God concerning those things which shall come hereafter, and the glory which shall follow after much tribulation. For after much tribulation come the blessings"—was followed by a chastisement: "I have selected my servant Edward Partridge, and have appointed unto him his mission in this land. But if he repent not of his sins, which are unbelief and blindness of heart, let him take heed lest he fall" (verse 15). He was told that his mission "to be a judge in Israel" was like those in Old Testament times—"to divide the land of the heritage of God unto his children" (verse 17)—and that he who "sitteth upon the judgment seat" should not "think he is ruler; but let God rule him that judgeth" (verse 20).

In verse 24 the Lord told Edward that "this is the land of his residence, and those whom he has appointed for his counselors [John Corrill and Isaac Morley]; and also . . . him whom I have appointed to keep my storehouse [Sidney Gilbert]." Then regarding their families, the Lord said they should "bring [them] to this land, as they shall counsel between themselves and me. For behold, it is not meet that I should command in all things" (verses 25–26).

John and Isaac returned to Kirtland to obtain their families. On August 9, Sidney Gilbert, William W. Phelps, Joseph, and eight others returned to Kirtland, arriving on August 27. Sidney commenced collecting and purchasing supplies, and when he returned to Independence in October 1831, he brought with him Keziah Keturah Rollins, who was his wife's sister, and her children, Mary and Caroline Rollins. (Sidney and Elizabeth had only one child, Loyal Gilbert, who lived for just a short time prior to their conversion.) In a letter to his wife, Lydia, in which he "broke the news that he wouldn't be returning to Ohio that summer," Edward Partridge asked that she and their five daughters join him in Missouri. He added that instead of being able to return to Ohio to help them move that fall, "Brother Gilbert or I must be here to attend the sales in Dec. [and] not knowing that he can get back by that time I have thought it advisable to stay here for the present contrary to [my] expectations." He then cautioned Lydia, "We have to suffer [and] shall for some time many privations here which you [and] I have not been much used to for year[s]."[167] To her credit, Lydia willingly packed up her home and their five daughters and joined Edward in Missouri.

Following the direction that "the disciples . . . should open their hearts, even to purchase this whole region of country" (Doctrine and Covenants 58:52), Edward began making land purchases in anticipation of the gathering of the Saints to Missouri. Much of that land was in Kaw Township west of Independence, but on August 8, 1831, he purchased lot 76 in Independence, where the "house of the printing" (verse 37) was to be built. Levi Hancock was a skilled brick mason and soon had built a two-story building that would house the Phelps family on the main floor and the printing office on the second floor, including exterior access via an outdoor stairway. At a conference back in Kirtland following his return, William W. Phelps was directed to purchase a printing press in Cincinnati as he returned to Missouri with his family. Printing of the monthly newspaper *The Evening and the Morning Star* and a weekly advertiser began in early 1832 following the purchase of paper and other printing supplies.

Martin Harris was commanded to "be an example unto the church, in laying [consecrating] his moneys before the bishop of the church" (verse 35), which was an expectation "unto every man that cometh in unto this land to receive an inheritance . . . according as the law [section 42] directs" (verse 36). There were restrictions, however, as to the number of the Saints who were to come to Zion. To most of the missionaries, the Lord said, "The time has not come for many years, for them to receive their inheritance in this land" (verse 44). He also directed, "Let the work of the gathering be not in haste nor by flight; but let it be done as it shall be counseled by the elders of the church at the conferences" (verse 56). He later promised that the Prophet would receive "power that he shall be enabled to discern by the spirit those who shall go up into the land of Zion" (Doctrine and Covenants 63:41). Unfortunately, as time passed, the expulsion of the Saints from Zion came in part because many arrived without authorization and did not acquire the land in the manner the Lord specified, resulting in the Missourians becoming concerned about being overrun and the Lord being displeased about their failure to obey.

Sidney Rigdon was commanded to "consecrate and dedicate this land, and the spot for the temple, unto the Lord" (Doctrine and Covenants 58:57), and the next day, "the land of Zion was consecrated and dedicated for the gathering of the Saints by Elder Rigdon."[168] That same day, twelve men (in honor of the twelve tribes of Israel), five of them from the Colesville Branch, laid the first log "as a foundation of Zion in Kaw township, twelve miles west of Independence."[169] As part of the service, Sidney asked his listeners, "'Do you pledge yourselves to keep the laws of God on this land, which you never have kept in your own lands?' [The audience responded,] we do. 'Do you pledge yourselves to see that others of your brethren who shall come hither do keep the laws of God?' [Those present again said,] we do. After [the dedicatory] prayer [Sidney] arose and said, 'I now pronounce this land consecrated and dedicated to the Lord for a possession and inheritance for the Saints (in the name of Jesus Christ, having authority from him). And for all the faithful servants of the Lord to the remotest ages of time. Amen.'"[170]

The following day, August 3, Joseph and seven other elders "assembled together where the temple is to be erected" (Doctrine and Covenants 57:1) just west of Independence. Following a reading of Psalm 87, which speaks of the glory and majesty of Zion, "Joseph Smith Jr. laid a stone at the northeast corner of the contemplated Temple in the name of the Lord Jesus of Nazareth"[171] and dedicated the temple site by prayer. He reported that "the scene was solemn and impressive."[172]

The Lord had also directed that "a conference meeting be called" (verse 58), so on August 4, Joseph held the first conference in Zion, with fourteen elders and the Colesville Saints, in Kaw Township at the home of Joshua and Margaret Kelsey Lewis, who had been among the few converts made by the Lamanite missionaries. The Lord had revealed in Doctrine and Covenants 58 that one item of business was to be conducted at the conference: taking away "that which has been bestowed upon Ziba [Peterson]," probably his priesthood office of elder, so that he would only "stand as a member in the Church" (verse 60). Although the revelation or the minutes do not record the reason, his offense may have involved breaking an engagement to marry.[173] Those minutes also record the "Confession of br. Ziba Peterson of his transgressions which were satisfactory to the Church as appeared by unanimous vote."[174] Ziba was reordained in an October 1832 Missouri conference. In addition to hearing Peterson's confession of his "transgressions," Sidney admonished the Saints to obey every requirement of heaven, and the sacrament was administered.

Instructing the Saints on the Sabbath: Section 59

The Prophet wrote that on August 7, "I attended the funeral of sister Polly [Peck] Knight, the wife of Joseph Knight Sen. This was the first death in the church in this land, and I can say a worthy member sleeps in Jesus till the resurrection. I also received the following," referring to the revelation now recorded in Doctrine and Covenants 59. The Knights played an important role in the Restoration. For example, the Prophet was employed by the Knights as well as Josiah Stowell while he courted Emma Hale. Likewise, he used Joseph Knight's wagon when he and Emma obtained the plates and the Urim and Thummim, and on more than one occasion, their help in supplying food and other supplies (including writing materials) enabled the Prophet to translate a major portion of the Book of Mormon while in Harmony. The Knight family served as the backbone of the original Colesville Branch.

Polly was in poor health when her family responded to the call to "go to the Ohio" (Doctrine and Covenants 37:1, 3; 38:32), and her health was failing when the Lord instructed the Colesville Saints to migrate to Zion when they were forced off Leman Copley's property (see Doctrine and Covenants 54:7–8). However, Polly's desire to see Zion outweighed her need to protect what little health she had remaining, causing her to refuse to be left behind in Ohio. As her son Newel described it, "Her only, or her greatest desire, was to set her feet upon the land of Zion, and to have her body interred in that land." Her condition was so poor that at one point, Newel left the boat they were traveling on and bought some wood to fashion a coffin. He added that "the Lord gave her the desire of her heart, and she lived to stand upon that land."[175] Polly died twelve days after her arrival in Zion and was the first Latter-day Saint to be buried in Missouri. It was especially about Polly that the Lord said, "Blessed . . . are they who have come up unto this land with an eye single to my glory, according to my commandments. For those that live shall inherit the earth, and those that die shall rest from all their labors, and their works shall follow them; and they shall receive a crown in the mansions of my Father, which I have prepared for them" (Doctrine and Covenants 59:1–2).

"Early members characterized this revelation as 'instructing the Saints how to keep the sabbath and how to fast and pray'" (Doctrine and Covenants 59, section heading). Prominent among the cultural differences between the early settlers and the Saints was their view of the Sabbath. William W. Phelps wrote that the Jackson County residents were "emigrants from Tennessee, Kentucky, Virginia, and the Carolinas, &c., with customs, manners, modes of living and a climate entirely different from the northerners."[176] The Prophet later wrote that many of the Jackson County residents were "the basest of men" who "had fled from the face of civilized society, to the frontier country to escape the hand of justice, in their midnight revels, their sabbath breaking, horseracing, and gambling."[177] One missionary from another Christian faith remarked, "Christian Sabbath observance here appears to be unknown. It is a day for merchandising, jollity, drinking, gambling, and general anti-Christian conduct."[178]

Although not specifically mentioned in "the Law" (Doctrine and Covenants 42), Sabbath day observance was an important aspect of worship to early converts.[179] Many converts to the Church brought their fairly strict approach to Sabbath observance with them as they joined the Saints. It is widely conjectured that the lack of Sabbath observance among the early settlers of Jackson County influenced the Prophet to inquire of the Lord concerning the matter. Therefore, the Lord said that the Saints should "offer a sacrifice unto the Lord . . . of a broken heart and a contrite spirit" (Doctrine and Covenants 59:8). He then indicated the means for that offering—"thou shalt go to the house of prayer and offer up thy sacraments upon my holy day" (verse 9)—and its attendant blessing—"that thou mayest more fully keep thyself unspotted from the world" (verse 9). Then, referring to a doctrine Joseph had learned about in Moroni 7:3 regarding "the rest of the Lord," the revelation emphasized that "this is a day appointed unto you to rest from your labors, and to pay thy devotions unto the Most High" (verse 10).

Other truths contained in Doctrine and Covenants 59 may be a continuation of the Lord's answer to the concerns of the early missionaries and settlers of Zion in section 57 about the "unsettled" condition of the early Independence settlement. As mentioned earlier, one visitor characterized Independence as having only "two or three merchants stores, and fifteen or twenty dwelling houses, built mostly of logs hewed on both sides."[180] In contrast, the Lord promised that if the Saints observed the Sabbath and to "do these things with thanksgiving, with cheerful hearts and countenances" (verse 15), great blessings would be theirs: "The fulness of the earth is yours. . . . The good things which come of the earth, whether for food or for raiment, or for houses, or for barns, or for orchards, or for gardens, or for vineyards; Yea, all things which come of the earth . . . are made for the benefit and the use of man" (verses 16–18). Revealing His motives, the Lord went on to say that it "pleaseth God that he hath given all these things unto man; for unto this end were they made to be used" (verse 20).

Returning to Ohio: Section 60

Following the events of the previous days, at least some of the missionaries in Missouri were anxious to return to their families. Ezra Boothe wrote, "Finding but little or no business for us to accomplish" once this work was done, "most of us became anxious to return home."[181] The Prophet himself recorded that the elders asked him "what they were to do."[182]

In the beginning of Doctrine and Covenants 60, the Lord spoke to those "who are to return speedily to the land from whence they came: Behold, it pleaseth me, that you have come up hither" (verse 1). However, He was also concerned: "But with some I am not well pleased, for they will not open their mouths, but they hide the talent which I have given unto them, because of the fear of man" (verse 2). Although much of Ezra's recollections were written after he left the Church, his characterization of the elders provides an explanation for the Lord's displeasure. "For more than two weeks, while I remained there [in Missouri], the disposition of the Elders appeared to be averse to preaching."[183]

Following more chastisement, the Lord spoke "concerning your journey unto the land from whence you came," indicating they were to travel east across the state on the Missouri River "for the place which is called St. Louis" (verse 5). He said they could make their own watercraft or purchase them "as seemeth you good, it mattereth not unto me" (verse 5), similar to His earlier directions to Edward Partridge and his counselors about bringing their families to Missouri "as they shall counsel between themselves and me" (Doctrine and Covenants 58:25). From there, Joseph, Oliver, and Sidney were to continue down the Mississippi River "for Cincinnati" (verse 6), where they were to "lift up their voice and declare my word with loud voices" (verse 7). The others were to "take their journey from St. Louis, two by two, and preach the word, not in haste, among the congregations of the wicked . . . until they return to the churches from whence they came" (verse 8).

The Lord said that Bishop Partridge was to "impart of the money which I have given him [moneys consecrated to the church], a portion unto mine elders who are commanded to return" (verse 10), in order to aid them in their journeys home. Then, if able, they were to pay the money back "by the way of the agent" (verse 11), Sidney Gilbert, who was also returning to Kirtland before returning back to Missouri.

A Vision of the Destroyer: Section 61

Joseph Smith, Sidney Rigdon, Oliver Cowdery, Peter Whitmer Jr., and Frederick G. Williams (who had joined the other four in Kirtland) left Independence by canoe on August 9, 1831, along with six other missionaries traveling on the Missouri River. They spent their first night at Fort Osage where they "had an excellent wild turkey for supper"[184] before continuing on the river the next day. The Missouri River traverses the width of the state of Missouri. It bends north on the west to form the borders between Missouri and Kansas and between Iowa and Nebraska and joins the Mississippi River on the east. This "River Distruction"[185] was widely known as a dangerous waterway that was only navigable three months of the year because of its "ever-varying channel"[186] that was full of sawyers (submerged trees anchored to the bottom of the river).

On the third day of the journey, "a spirit of animosity and discord" affected the group. Ezra Boothe recorded that "the conduct of the Elders became very displeasing to Oliver Cowdery," causing Oliver to prophesy, "As the Lord God liveth, if you do not behave better, some accident will befall you."[187] Later, the canoe carrying Joseph and Sidney Rigdon was nearly capsized by a sawyer. Frustrated by the conduct of the group and no doubt unnerved by his own near-death experience, Joseph instructed them to disembark and camp for the night at McIlwaine's Bend (now Miami) on the north side of the river, causing some of the men to call him a coward. They set up camp and then met together to address the contention. Some of the elders expressed their displeasure about Oliver's warning, and some added to the criticism of Joseph by accusing him of being "quite dictatorial,"[188] to which Joseph took offense. The meeting continued well past midnight before everyone reconciled.

The following morning, the Prophet recorded that William W. Phelps, "in open vision by daylight, saw the destroyer in his most horrible power, ride upon the face of the waters; others heard the noise, but saw not the vision." Joseph also recorded, "The next morning after prayer, I received the following." [189]Apparently referring to the previous days' contentions and the brethren's efforts to reconcile, the Lord said their "sins were now forgiven" (Doctrine and Covenants 61:2). "I, the Lord, was angry with you yesterday, but today mine anger is turned away" (verse 20). Indeed, Joseph was inspired to delay their journeying: "I would not suffer that ye should part until you were chastened for all your sins, that you might be one, that you might not perish in wickedness" (verse 8).

He also indicated that He only allowed the group "to be moving swiftly upon the waters, whilst the inhabitants on either side are perishing in unbelief" (verse 3) so that they "might bear record" of the "many dangers upon the waters . . . especially upon these waters" (verses 4–5), so that the Saints who would be traveling to Zion would "come not in journeying upon them" (verse 18). In fact, those who were "commanded to journey and go up unto the land of Zion" (verse 24) in the future were not to "come upon the waters to journey, save upon the [Ohio Erie] canal" (verse 23).

Having allowed the brethren to temporarily ignore the fact that the nearby inhabitants were "perishing in unbelief" (verse 3), the Lord said, "It behooveth me that ye should part" (verse 9), and He gave specific instructions as to how the brethren were to return to Kirtland. Sidney Gilbert and William W. Phelps were to continue foregoing missionary duties and "take their journey in haste that they may fill their mission" (verse 9) (i.e., stop in Cincinnati to obtain a printing press). Similarly, Sidney Rigdon, Joseph Smith, and Oliver Cowdery were not to "open their mouths in the congregations of the wicked until they arrive at Cincinnati; And in that place they shall lift up their voices unto God against that people, yea, unto him whose anger is kindled against their wickedness, a people who are well-nigh ripened for destruction" (verses 30–31). Then these three were to "journey for the congregations of their brethren [back in Ohio], for their labors even now are wanted more abundantly among them than among the congregations of the wicked" (verse 32). Therefore, following these divine directions, they traveled overland to St. Louis and journeyed by stagecoach to Kirtland by way of Cincinnati.

Concerning the "residue" of the missionaries, the Lord said, "Let them journey and declare the word among the congregations of the wicked" (verse 33) as they had been commanded on their journey to Missouri. All but two were allowed to select their companions "as seemeth them good," except "my servant Reynolds Cahoon, and my servant Samuel H. Smith, with whom I am well pleased," who were to "be not separated until they return to their homes, and this for a wise purpose in me" (verse 35). The Lord did not provide additional detail about His "wise purpose" for directing Reynolds and Samuel to continue their mission as companions, but Reynolds' description of their journey back to Kirtland is enlightening:

> We then traveled on the Greene County Indiana and on Monday evening August 29th arrived in the region of country where we had held meetings [on their way to Missouri]. On our westward journeys we found the people glad to see us. Again on Tuesday August 30th we preached at the residence of Mr. Lemon where we held three meetings. We found this whole region a country in a state of excitement over the Book of Mormon. The people were searching the scriptures. Some of them had read their Bibles through twice

since we last visited them and as soon as they heard that we had
returned they were all ready to come together to hear what further
testimony we had to give. A number of them acknowledged their
belief in the work. Others said they could find no objection to it and
were anxious to receive a testimony in regard to its truth.[190]

Their labors in Greene County resulted in six baptisms, two priesthood ordinations, and the establishment of a branch.

A Divinely Orchestrated Missionary Reunion: Section 62

As indicated, because of the command to "preach by the way,"
not all the missionaries arrived in Jackson County at the same time.
Hyrum Smith and John Murdock had been instructed to "take their
journey . . . by the way of Detroit" (Doctrine and Covenants 52:8)
and were delayed a week in Chariton, Missouri, in early August when
John fell ill. There they were joined by David Whitmer and Harvey
Whitlock, and on August 13, the Prophet's group arrived at Chariton
and found these four missionaries. Joseph recorded that "after the joyful salutations with which brethren meet each other,"[191] he dictated the
revelation now found in Doctrine and Covenants 62.

The Lord indicated that He was very much aware of those "who
have not as yet gone up unto the land of Zion" (verse 2), and the fact
that the two companionships and Joseph's group had seemingly met
each other by chance had actually been orchestrated by Him: "I, the
Lord, have brought you together . . . that the faithful among you should
be preserved and rejoice together in the land of Missouri" (verse 6).
Although their "mission [was] not yet full" (verse 2), He acknowledged
their efforts up to that point, saying that the testimonies they had borne
were "recorded in heaven for the angels to look upon" (verse 3) and that
their sins were forgiven. They were to continue their journey to "the
land of Zion" (verse 4), where they were to hold a sacrament meeting
(see also Doctrine and Covenants 58:61), then "return to bear record"
(verse 5). He also allowed them some options as to the size of their
companionships—"altogether, or two by two, as seemeth you good"
(verse 5)—and their means of travel—"upon horses, or upon mules,
or in chariots" (verse 7)—according to "judgment and the directions

of the Spirit" (verse 8). John Murdock had not fully recovered, so the four missionaries bought a horse for him to ride, and the four of them traveled together.[192]

When Joseph arrived in Ohio on August 27, he learned that "in the absence of the Elders many apostitized,"[193] prompting him to visit congregations in Ohio in order to provide "much exhortation."[194] In many cases, including among some of the recently returned Missouri missionaries, the Church members had engaged in behavior that warranted Church discipline, which was attended to in conferences in early September.

In addition to some of the examples described above of how some of the missionaries were "exceedingly blessed even above measure" (Doctrine and Covenants 58:61), there is also the inspiring story of William E. McLellin's conversion. It began when two different pairs of missionaries preached in Paris, Illinois, where William lived. Samuel Smith and Reynolds Cahoon were the first. They held an evening meeting describing the coming forth of the Book of Mormon and then left the next morning. William depicted his next missionary encounter in the following letter:

> But in a few days two others [Elders David Whitmer and Harvey Whitlock] came into the neighborhood proclaiming that these were the last days, and that God had sent forth the Book of Mormon to show the times of the fulfillment of the ancient prophecies, when the Savior shall come to destroy iniquity off the face of the earth and reign with his Saints in Millennial Rest. One of these was a witness to the book and had seen an angel, which declared its truth. . . . They were in the neighborhood about a week. I talked much with them by way of enquiry and argument. They believed Joseph Smith to be an inspired prophet. They told me that he and between 20 & thirty [of] their preachers were on their way to Independence. My curiosity was roused up and my anxiety also to know the truth.[195]

On July 30 William closed the school where he was teaching and went with David and Harvey as far as Shelby County, Illinois. After visiting with his brother and an uncle at Springfield, he continued on to Independence, where he met and was baptized by Hyrum Smith.

Chapter 11

"The Day Cometh That All Things Shall Be Subject unto Me": More Guidance for Zion from the Morleys' Farm

Doctrine and Covenants 63–64

Chronological Summary

- June 19, 1831—Joseph Smith and a company of others leave for Missouri
- July 14—Joseph Smith and his company arrive in Jackson County, Missouri
- August 27—Joseph Smith and his company arrive in Kirtland
- August 30—Doctrine and Covenants 63 is revealed
- August 31—An unpublished revelation is received
- September 11—Doctrine and Covenants 64 is revealed
- September 12—Joseph and Emma Smith move from the Morley farm to the John and Alice Johnson farm in Hiram, Ohio

Further Instructions on Gathering to Zion: Section 63

Following the arrival of Joseph Smith, Oliver Cowdery, and Sidney Rigdon from Missouri three days earlier, on August 30, 1831, the Lord spoke to the Prophet about the gathering of the Saints to Missouri. There were several questions yet to be answered regarding the gathering of the Saints to Zion, despite the fact that "the land of Zion was the most important temporal object"[196] to members of the Church and that the Lord had identified Jackson County, Missouri, as the location for Zion (see Doctrine and Covenants 57:3). The Lord had directed the Saints to purchase lands there (see Doctrine and Covenants 57:4), and an epistle was to "be presented unto all the churches to obtain moneys, to be put into the hands of the bishop" (Doctrine and Covenants 58:51), but more direction was needed as to how to carry out this command.

Doctrine and Covenants 58 also indicated that at least for many of the Saints, "the time has not yet come for many years, for them to receive their inheritance" (verse 44), and that "the work of the gathering be not in haste, nor by flight; but let it be done as it shall be counseled by the elders of the church" (verse 56), thus leaving Joseph and others unsure as to how exactly to determine who would gather and when. Also, as mentioned earlier, when Joseph arrived in Ohio on August 27, he learned that "in the absence of the Elders many apostitized," causing him to visit congregations in Ohio in order to provide "much exhortation."[197] This caused Joseph to write, "We could not help beholding the exertions of Satan to blind the eyes of the people so as to hide the true light that lights every man that comes into the world."[198]

The word of the Lord revealed to assist in dealing with these matters—now known as Doctrine and Covenants 63—must have been a welcome source of encouragement for Joseph and those from whom he sought counsel. The Lord first gave directions about apostasy among the members of the Church, stating, "I, the Lord, utter my voice, and it shall be obeyed. Wherefore . . . let the wicked take heed, and let the rebellious fear and tremble" (verses 5–6). He singled out those who "seeketh signs . . . but not unto salvation" (verse 7) and "adulterers and adulteresses; some of whom have turned away from you, and others [who] remain with you that hereafter shall be revealed" (verse 14).

Regarding who should gather to Zion, the Lord reiterated that the Saints "should assemble themselves together unto the land of Zion, not in haste, lest there should be confusion" (verse 24), and that He would "give unto my servant Joseph Smith, Jun., power that he shall be enabled to discern by the Spirit those who shall go up unto the land of Zion, and those of my disciples who shall tarry" (verse 41). He also reminded the Saints that they should "purchase the lands" for the gathering in Zion (verse 27), then specifically directed that the disciples "who dwell upon this [Morley] farm"—the Saints who gathered there from New York, including Joseph and Emma, as well other converts who were original members of the Morley "Family" (i.e., those who gathered there to have "all things common")—should "arrange their temporal concerns" (verse 38) because Titus Billings, Isaac and Lucy Morley's brother-in-law, was to "dispose of the land [Morley farm]" (verse 39). This consecration of Isaac and Lucy was to be part of the "moneys . . . sent up unto the land of Zion" for the Saints "whom I have appointed to receive" inheritances there (verse 40). Newel K. Whitney was to "retain his store . . . yet for a little season" but was also directed to "impart all the money which he can impart, to be sent up unto the land of Zion" (verses 42–43). Newel was to now "speedily visit the "churches" (branches) in Ohio and elsewhere "for obtaining moneys even as I have directed" (verse 46).

An Unpublished Revelation Directing
Three Brethren to Travel to Zion

A day after section 63 was received, the Lord spoke to the Prophet again, probably on the Morley farm, directing three brethren—John Burk, Erastus Babbitt, and David Elliott—to travel to Zion in the subsequent months. Although lacking in detail as to the nature and permanency of the assignment, it may have been related to the August 1 revelation given in Missouri stating in part, "Inasmuch as there is land obtained, let there be workmen sent forth of all kinds unto this land, to labor for the saints of God" (Doctrine and Covenants 58:54). All three had skills that were invaluable to the Zion Saints—Erastus was a carpenter and millwright, David was a blacksmith, and John may have had some experience working in sawmills—and this end-of-August revelation was a fulfilment of the promise the Lord gave the Prophet that He would give him "power that he shall be enabled to discern by the Spirit those who shall go up unto the land of Zion" (Doctrine and Covenants 63:41). Unfortunately, these brethren were slow to act. Historical records indicate that five months later, Oliver Cowdery requested that two of them, Erastus and David, move to Missouri. John eventually moved to Clay County but probably not until 1833 or 1834; David didn't move until 1838, well after the Saints started gathering to Caldwell and Daviess counties; and Erastus never went.

More Direction for Specific Individuals: Section 64

Besides the contentions that occurred while the Missouri missionaries were traveling home in August 1831, there was also an argument between Edward Partridge and Joseph, witnessed by Ezra Booth, about the quality of land being considered for purchase in Zion. Continuing to not allow for the Prophet's humanity, Ezra added this experience to his growing list of rationalizations for leaving the Church. Contrary to Ezra's perspective, Sidney Rigdon faulted Edward, indicating that he had "insulted the Lord's prophet in particular and assumed authority over him in open violation of the Laws of God."[199] Ezra further rationalized that if Joseph and others could travel back to Ohio without walking to facilitate preaching "by the way" (Doctrine and Covenants 52:23) and "not in haste" (Doctrine and Covenants 52:8), so could he and Isaac Morley, his companion.

Isaac and Lucy Morley had been directed to consecrate their farm and move to Missouri (see Doctrine and Covenants 64:20). On September 11, Joseph and Emma were preparing to move to Hiram to live with the Johnsons when on that same day, the Lord revealed further commandments relative to Zion in the section now numbered as Doctrine and Covenants 64. He acknowledged that Joseph had "sinned" but had been forgiven (verses 6 and 7), that "the keys of the mysteries of the kingdom shall not be taken from" him (verse 5), and that there were brethren "who have sought occasion against him without cause" (verse 6). After speaking of the doctrine of forgiveness, the Lord singled out Ezra Booth and Isaac Morley because they "kept not the law, neither the commandments; they sought evil in their hearts," referring to their chosen mode of transportation back to Ohio and because "they condemned for evil that thing in which there was no evil" (verses 15–16). Isaac repented and went on to a lifetime of faithful service in the kingdom. Ezra's story was different.

The Lord also singled out Edward Partridge, saying, "He hath sinned . . . but when these things are made known unto them, and they repent of the evil, they shall be forgiven" (verse 17). John Whitmer recorded Edward's response: "If Br. Joseph has not forgiven him he hopes he will, as he is & has always been sorry."[200] On the other hand, Ezra, who had been barred from preaching as an elder at a conference five days earlier, went on to become even more angry and one of the most infamous anti–Latter-day Saints in history.[201]

Frederick G. Williams had joined with the original four Lamanite missionaries in November 1830 following his conversion. Perhaps surprisingly, the Lord told him, "I will not that [he] . . . should sell his farm, for I, the Lord, will to retain a strong hold in the land of Kirtland, for the space of five years" (verse 21). Interestingly, five years from that revelation marked the year Joseph called the "Pentecostal" season (i.e., the year during which numerous revelatory blessings were enjoyed by the Saints as the Kirtland Temple was completed). Those years saw Frederick become a scribe for Joseph and later the second counselor in the First Presidency.

Sidney Gilbert was to "return upon his business, and to his agency in the land of Zion" (verse 18). However, Sidney and Newel K. Whitney were not to "sell their store and their possessions" in Kirtland, a direction repeated from the previous section that provided important financial strength for the Church there "until the residue of the church, which remaineth in this place, shall go up unto the land of Zion" (verse 18). This migration occurred in 1838 when the bulk of the Kirtland Saints joined the Missouri Saints in Caldwell and Daviess counties.

The long-term result of obeying this direction was that the Lord would "provide for his saints . . . that they may obtain an inheritance in the land of Zion" (verse 30). Then, in the remaining verses, the Lord reminded the Saints of the future glory of Zion, all the while reiterating that "all things must come to pass in their time. Wherefore, be not weary in well-doing, for ye are laying the foundation of a great work. And out of small things proceedeth that which is great" (verses 32–33). At that future date, "Zion shall flourish, and the glory of the Lord shall be upon her; And she shall be an ensign unto the people, and there shall come unto her out of every nation under heaven. And . . . the nations of the earth shall tremble because of her" (verses 41–43).

Chapter 12

"Go and Preach My Gospel Which Ye Have Received": Leman Copley and the Mission to the Shakers

Doctrine and Covenants 49

Chronological Summary

- By 1831—Leman Copley is baptized
- February 1831—Leman offers his property (in Thompson, Ohio) as a place for Joseph and Emma to reside (though the Lord directed them to the Morley farm instead)
- March—Leman agreed to allow the Colesville Saints to move onto his property
- May 7—Sidney Rigdon, Parley P. Pratt, and Leman Copley are called to preach to the Shaker colony (Doctrine and Covenants 49)
- About May 16—The Colesville Saints move onto Leman's property

- May 20—Joseph receives a revelation in Thompson provid-
  ing arrangements for the settlement of the New York Saints
  in Ohio according to the law of consecration (Doctrine and
  Covenants 51)
- By June—Leman rescinds his offer and orders the Saints off
  his property
- June 10—The Lord directs the Colesville Saints to move to
  Missouri (Doctrine and Covenants 54)

Leman Copley was an early Ohio convert who played an interesting
role in the early Restoration—not because of a prominent position or
major contribution but because of a few decisions he made that affected
a large number of Saints and because the Lord chose to reveal important doctrines related to those decisions. At some point before his conversion, he had joined with the United Society of Believers in Christ's
Second Appearing, otherwise known as the "Shaking Quakers" or simply "Shakers" because of the demonstrative shaking they engaged in
when they thought they were under the influence of the Holy Ghost.
The sect had its beginnings in England, after which many of its adher-
ents left for America under the direction of their "spiritual mother,"
Ann Lee, to escape persecution. Around the time of Joseph and Emma
Smith's arrival in Ohio (about February 4, 1831), Leman offered his
home as a place for them to reside, but the Lord had directed that the
Church build them a home on the Morley farm (see Doctrine and
Covenants 41:7).

The first contact between the Saints and the Shakers occurred
when the four Lamanite missionaries visited the Shaker community in
North Union, eighteen miles from Kirtland, in November 1830. The
presiding Shaker elder, Ashbell Kitchell, wrote in his journal that their
work in Ohio "created a good deal of excitement among the people.
They stated they had received a New Revelation, had seen an angel,
and had been instructed into many things in relation to the history of
America, that was not known before."[202]

In their visit to "the Believers," Ashbell wrote, "One by the name
of Oliver Lowdree [Cowdery] . . . stated that he had been one who had
been an assistant in the translation of the golden Bible, and had also
seen the angel, and had been commissioned by him to go out and bear

testimony." They were allowed to preach for "two nights & one day" while they "tarried with [them]," but the Shakers concluded that the missionaries "had nothing for us, [but] we treated them kindly, and labored to find out what manner of spirit they were of. They appeared meek and mild; but as for light, or knowledge of the way of God, I considered them very ignorant of Christ or his work; therefore I treated them with the tenderness of children."[203]

The missionaries apparently left seven copies of the Book of Mormon with the Shakers, "but they were soon returned as not interesting enough to keep them awake while reading. After some months they called for them and took them away, except one which was given me a present. They appeared to have full faith in the virtue of their books, that whoever would read them, would feel so thoroughly convinced of the truth of what they contained, that they would be unable to resist."[204]

Despite his characterization of the Shakers' reaction to the Book of Mormon, Ashbell wrote:

I believed that I should one day have to meet them and decide the matter; and, least I should do anything that should injure the cause of God, or bring weakness on myself I wrote home for council [sic] but could obtain none, for the case was new and none were acquainted with it in the Church, therefore they could give no council, and they left me to exercise my judgment. For some time I felt some straitened, not knowing what course to take. At length I concluded that I was dedicated and entirely devoted to God, and desired to do what was right; that if God had any hand in that work, he would inform me by some means, that I might know what to do, either by letting me have an interview with the angel, or by some other means give me knowledge of my duty.

In this situation I remained for a long time, occasionally hearing that they expected to come after a while and lead us into the water. We continued on friendly terms in the way of trade and other acts of good neighborship until the spring of 1831 when we were visited on Saturday evening by Sidney Rigdon and Leman Copley, the latter of whom had been among us; but not liking the cross any too well [an allusion to the Shaker belief in absolute celibacy], had taken up with

Mormonism as the easier plan and had been appointed by them as one of the missionaries to convert us.[205]

Leman must have also been highly influenced. The Prophet described him as "apparently honest hearted" but characterized his conversion in saying that he "still retained ideas that the Shakers were right in some particulars of their faith."[206] Discussions around those ideas probably led to the revelation now contained in Doctrine and Covenants 49 because Joseph indicated that "in order to have more perfect understanding on the subject, I inquired of the Lord and received [section 49]."[207] John Whitmer added that Leman already possessed an anxiety "that some of the elders should go to his former brethren and preach the gospel."[208]

In the revelation, the Lord directed Sidney Rigdon, Parley P. Pratt, and Leman Copley to "go and preach my gospel . . . unto the Shakers" (verse 1), whom the Lord described as wanting to "know the truth in part, but not all" (verse 2). The Lord specifically commanded Leman that he should "reason with them" but "not according to that which he has received of them, but according to that which shall be taught him by you my servants" (verse 4). "That which he has received of them" included the belief that "Christ's Second Coming had already occurred and that He had appeared in the form of a woman, Ann Lee. They did not consider baptism by water essential. They rejected marriage and believed in a life of total celibacy. Some Shakers also forbade the eating of meat" (Doctrine and Covenants 49, section heading).

The Lord addressed each of the Shakers' doctrinal misconceptions. He said that He "now reigneth in the heavens, and will reign till he descends on the earth . . . but the hour and the day no man knoweth" (verses 6–7). Continuing in that same vein later in the revelation, He said, "Wherefore, be not deceived, but continue in steadfastness, looking forth for the heavens to be shaken, and the earth to tremble . . . when the angels shall sound his trumpet. . . . But before the great day of the Lord shall come, Jacob shall flourish in the wilderness, and the Lamanites shall blossom as the rose. Zion shall flourish upon the hills and rejoice upon the mountains, and shall be assembled together unto the place which I have appointed" (verses 23–25). He also reiterated the command to "repent and be baptized in the name of Jesus Christ" (verse 13) and the divine origin of marriage: "Whoso forbiddeth to marry is not ordained of God, for marriage is ordained of God unto man" (verse 15). Likewise, regarding meat, "whoso forbiddeth to abstain from meats . . . is not ordained of God" (verse 18).

Sidney and Leman spent the night debating with Ashbell. Ashbell concluded, "We found that the life of self-denial corresponded better with the life of Christ, than Mormonism." Sidney argued against "bearing the cross," so Ashbell told him, "I could not look on him as a Christian. Thus the matter stood and we retired to rest, not knowing that they had then in possession what they called a revelation or message from Jesus Christ to us, which they intended to deliver [the next day] and which they supposed would bring us to terms."[209]

Having spent the night there, Sidney and Leman continued in conversing with the Shakers about doctrinal differences, all the while maintaining a somewhat friendly tone that had characterized their interactions the night before. Then at some point Ashbell recommended that neither side "force their doctrine on the other at this time; but let the time be spent in feeling of the spirit." His hope was that Sidney would have a change of heart regarding the restored gospel—that he might "yet see that the foundation he was now on, was sandy, . . . and if he should, he might desire to find a resting place—something substantial to place his feet on, where he would be safe."[210]

The Shakers proceeded with their usual Sabbath meeting, which Sidney, Leman, and Parley attended. As the end of the meeting was announced, Sidney asked for and was given the opportunity to read the revelation. Afterward, Ashbell spoke for the whole congregation in saying, "The piece he had read, bore on its face, the image of its author; that the Christ that dictated that, I was well acquainted with, and had been, from a boy; that I had been much troubled to get rid of his influence, and I wished to have nothing more to do with him; and as for any gift he had authorized them to exercise among us, I would release them and their Christ from any further burden about us, and take all the responsibility on myself."[211] Not satisfied, Sidney asked for the other congregants to reply. Ashbell wrote, "They were fully satisfied with what they had, and wished to have nothing to do with either them or their Christ." Sidney was satisfied, but Parley "commenced shaking his coattail; he said he shook the dust from his garments as a testimony against us, that we had rejected the word of the Lord Jesus." Ashbell's patience had worn thin by then. "You filthy beast, dare you presume to come in here, and try to imitate a man of God by shaking your filthy tail; confess your sins and purge your soul from your lusts, and your other abominations before you ever presume to do the like again." He then turned to Leman, saying, "You hypocrite, you knew better; you knew where the living work of God was; but for the sake of indulgence, you could consent to deceive yourself and them, but you shall reap the fruit of your own doings."[212] Parley left immediately, Sidney left after staying for supper, and Leman left the next day.

Not long thereafter, Leman returned to North Union and "begged for union" with the Shakers. Ashbell wrote, "After some consultation we concluded to give him union, and help him through; and to accomplish this, I went home with him [to Thompson], and held a meeting in the dooryard, among the Mormons."[213] Ashbell stayed the night, then commenced a conversation with Newel Knight, the branch president, the next morning. In the course of the conversation, Ashbell said the following:

> [He] stirred the feelings of an old man, that proved to be the Elder's Father [Joseph Knight Sr.], which so raised the indignation of the Elder that he let on me his heaviest mettels [possibly "strength of temperament"]; he poured it on at the top of his voice, and wound up by informing me that unless I repented I should go to hell. I waited with patience until he was thro', and then asked him if he would hear me; to which he consented.
>
> I told him if the words he had spoken had come from a man of God they would have caused my knees to have smote together like Belshazers, but coming as they did from a man that lived in his lusts—who gratified a beastly propensity [another reference to the Shaker preference for celibacy] and often in a manner that was far below the beasts, and at the same time professing to be a follower of Christ, his words had no weight, but passed by me without making any impression. I then gave him a lecture on the subject of the cross, and a life of self-denial.[214]

Leman then ordered the Colesville Saints off his property, breaking the covenant of consecration he had made that allowed them to move there in the first place. He received Church disciplinary action shortly thereafter but was reinstated in October 1832, suggesting that if he did rejoin the Shakers, his commitment to them was short-lived. In 1834 he falsely testified against the Prophet in the lawsuit Joseph brought against Doctor Philastus Hurlbut for threatening his life.[215] Joseph later wrote, "[Leman Copley] confessed that he bore a false testimony against me in that suit, but verily thought, at the time, that he was right, but on calling to mind all the circumstances connected with the things that happened at that time, he was convinced that he was wrong, and humbly confessed it, and asked my forgiveness, which was readily granted. He also wished to be received into the Church again, by baptism, and was received according to his desire. He gave me his confession in writing."[216] However, when the Saints left Ohio for Missouri in 1838, Leman stayed behind. He may have been among the few Saints who remained in Kirtland but stayed connected to the Church, because like some of those, following the Prophet's martyrdom, he joined James C. Brewster and Hazen Aldrich and later Austin Cowles in their splinter groups.

Chapter 13

"A Babe on His Mother's Lap": A Miraculous Prophecy and the Gospel of Abraham

Doctrine and Covenants 132

Chronological Summary

- About February 4, 1831—Joseph and Emma Smith arrive in Kirtland
- March 1831— Joseph and Emma move to the Morley farm (living in the Morleys' home and then in their own home)
- About February–March 1831—Joseph translates the book of Genesis

In the section heading to Doctrine and Covenants 132 concerning the principle of plural marriage, it states, "Although the revelation was recorded in 1843, evidence indicates that some of the principles involved in this revelation were known by the Prophet as early as 1831." There is very little contemporary evidence of Joseph teaching this principle in 1831. Most testimonials come many years after the fact, and many of them contradict each other. However, the accounts that are recorded indicate that Joseph may have learned some of the principles involved in plural marriage when he stayed with the Whitneys at their home in Kirtland or during the time he lived on the Morley farm.

Accounts of Joseph Smith Introducing and Teaching Principles of Plural Marriage in 1831

In 1886 President Joseph F. Smith, then a member of the First Presidency, stated, "Plural marriage was first revealed to Joseph Smith in 1831, but being forbidden to make it public, or to teach it as a doctrine of the Gospel at that time, he confided the facts to only a very few of his intimate associates."[217] Joseph B. Noble, who practiced polygamy in Nauvoo, recalled in 1883 "that the Prophet Joseph told him that the doctrine of celestial marriage was revealed to him while he was engaged on the work of translation of the scriptures [Joseph Smith's revision of the Bible], but when the communication was first made, the Lord stated that the time for the practice of that principle had not arrived."[218] Historians cite that Joseph Smith was working on the translation of the Bible—specifically the book of Genesis—in February and March of 1831 and would have encountered the principle of polygamy with Abraham and Jacob.[219]

In 1861, in a letter to Brigham Young, William W. Phelps reflected on his experience traveling to Missouri with Joseph Smith in June 1831. He stated that during the group's encounters with various Native American groups, Joseph received a revelation that was never published instructing some of the men to marry Native American women. Phelps, referring to this unpublished revelation, wrote to Brigham Young, "About three years after this was given, I asked brother Joseph [Smith Jr.] privately, how 'we,' that were mentioned in the revelation could take wives from the 'natives'—as we were all married men? He replied instantly 'In th[e] same manner that Abraham took Hagar and Katurah [Keturah]; and Jacob took Rachel Bilhah and Zilpah: by revelation—the Saints of the Lord are always directed by revelation.'"[220]

"This Church Will Fill North and South America—It Will Fill the World"

For many years after the selling of the Morley farm in October 1831, the Church continued to use the public school house on the property for meetings and gatherings. One such gathering occurred on Sunday, April 27, 1834, just four days before the first group of brethren would leave for Missouri with Zion's Camp and just one day after the arrival of Wilford Woodruff to Kirtland. Wilford recorded the following event:

> On Sunday night the Prophet called on all who held the Priesthood to gather into the little log school house they had there. It was a small house, perhaps 14 feet square. But it held the whole of the Priesthood of the Church of Jesus Christ of Latter-day Saints who were then in the town of Kirtland, and who had gathered together to go off in Zion's camp. That was the first time I ever saw Oliver Cowdery, or heard him speak; the first time I ever saw Brigham Young and Heber C. Kimball, and the two Pratts, and Orson Hyde and many others. There were no Apostles in the Church then except Joseph Smith and Oliver Cowdery. When we got together the Prophet called upon the Elders of Israel with him to bear testimony of this work. Those that I have named spoke, and a good many that I have not named, bore their testimonies. When they got through the Prophet said, "Brethren I have been very much edified and instructed in your testimonies here tonight, but I want to say to you before the Lord, that you know no more concerning the destinies of this Church and kingdom than a babe upon its mother's lap. You don't comprehend it."
>
> I was rather surprised. He said "it is only a little handful of Priesthood you see here tonight, but this Church will fill North and South America—it will fill the world." Among other things he said, "it will fill the Rocky Mountains. There will be tens of thousands of Latter-day Saints who will be gathered in the Rocky Mountains, and there they will open the door for the establishing of the Gospel among the Lamanites, who will receive the Gospel and their endowments and the blessings of God. This people will go into the Rocky Mountains; they will there build temples to the Most High. They

will raise up a posterity there, and the Latter-day Saints who dwell in these mountains will stand in the flesh until the coming of the Son of Man. The Son of Man will come to them while in the Rocky Mountains."[221]

When this revelation was given to Joseph Smith, there were only a little more than 4,000 members of the Church, and the Saints were settling mostly in Ohio and Missouri.[222] There are no records discussing the possibility of moving west until the 1840s, and it wasn't until 1846 that the Council of Fifty decided that the Saints should move west of the Rocky Mountains.[223] At the end of 2022, the Church had a total membership of 16,805,400 members in 31,315 congregations throughout the world. The message of the restored gospel is currently being shared in 188 published languages.[224] In a small wood schoolhouse with only a small gathering of priesthood holders, Joseph the seer revealed great truths about the growth of the Church of Jesus Christ throughout the world.

NOTES

1. The revelations given on the Morley farm were not published until 1833, but mobs destroyed most of the fruits of that labor (known as the Book of Commandments). The first edition of the Doctrine and Covenants was published in 1835, but numerous reorganizations, renumberings, and so forth since then have produced that standard work in its current form. In this book, to aid in clarity, we will speak of revelations as their current section number, but we want to acknowledge that those numbers are of relatively modern origin.

2. Parley P. Pratt, *Autobiography of Parley P. Pratt* (Salt Lake City, UT: Deseret Book, 1985), 36–37.

3. "History of Joseph Smith," *Times and Seasons* 4, no. 19: 289–290.

4. Ezra Booth, "Letter IX," in E. D. Howe, *Mormonism Unvailed* (Painesville, OH: s.n., 1834), 217.

5. *Autobiography of Parley P. Pratt*, 38.

6. *Autobiography of Parley P. Pratt*, 50.

7. Orson F. Whitney, "The Aaronic Priesthood (Newel K. Whitney)," *Contributor* 6, no. 4 (Jan. 1885): 125. Although commonly cited, there is some concern among historians about the authenticity of the phrase "Thou art the man." See Mark Lyman Staker, "Newel K. Whitney: Thou Art the Man," *BYU Studies Quarterly* 42, no. 1 (2003): 131.

8. Elizabeth Ann Whitney, "A Leaf from an Autobiography, Continued," *Woman's Exponent* 7, no. 7 (Sept. 1878): 51.

9. Karl Ricks Anderson, "The Western Reserve," in *Mapping Mormonism*, ed. Brandon S. Plewe, S. Kent Brown, Donald Q. Cannon, and Richard H. Jackson (Provo, UT: BYU Press, 2012), 28–29.

10. Hattie Esplin, "History of Isaac Morley," FamilySearch, accessed Apr. 10, 2024, https://www.familysearch.org/service/records/storage/das-mem/patron/

v2/TH-904-50926-2137-14/dist.txt?ctx=ArtCtxPublic; Cordelia Morley Cox, "A Sketch of the Life of My Father, Isaac Morley, One of the Pioneers to Salt Lake Valley in 1848," Book of Abraham Project, accessed Apr. 10, 2024, http://boap.org/LDS/Early-Saints/IMorley.html; "Morley, Isaac," in Andrew Jenson, *Latter-day Saint Biographical Encyclopedia: A Compilation of Biographical Sketches of Prominent Men and Women in the Church of Jesus Christ of Latter-day Saints* (Salt Lake City, UT: Andrew Jenson History Co., 1901), 1:235, as referenced in "Morley, Isaac," The Joseph Smith Papers, accessed Apr. 10, 2024, https://www.josephsmithpapers.org/person/isaac-morley.

11. "Lucy Morley (Gunn)," Geni, accessed Apr. 10, 2024, https://www.geni.com/people/Lucy-Morley/6000000003682493400.

12. "Lucy Gunn," FamilySearch, accessed Apr. 10, 2024, https://ancestors.familysearch.org/en/KWVM-MGT/lucy-gunn-1786-1848. The Geni.com reference lists fourteen children, two of whom are listed only as "Son Morley Twin" and "Daughter Morley Twin."

13. Frank Prodmore, *Robert Owen: A Biography* (New York: D. Appleton & Company, 1907).

14. Titus Billings was Isaac Morley's brother-in-law. He was born in Massachusetts and earned his livelihood as a stonemason, carpenter, and musician. He moved to Mentor, Geauga County, Ohio, by 1817 and married Diantha Morley, Isaac's sister, that same year. They were Campbellites, then joined The Church of Jesus Christ of Latter-day Saints in 1830 in Kirtland. Titus was ordained a deacon by October 1831 and moved his family to Jackson County in 1832, where he was ordained an elder by Thomas B. Marsh. He moved his family to Clay County when the Saints were driven out of Jackson County, then moved back to Kirtland probably in 1835 where he worked on the Kirtland Temple.

   The Billings moved to Caldwell County, Missouri, by 1837, where he was ordained a high priest by Edward Partridge and Isaac Morley on August 1, 1837. He was called as a counselor to Bishop Edward Partridge in 1837 and served until 1840. Titus fought in the Battle of Crooked River in 1838, then was among the first to move his family to Illinois (Lima, Adams County) that same year. The following year they moved to Yelrome ("Morley" spelled backward) near Nauvoo, where Titus served on the Yelrome high council until 1845. He was appointed colonel in the Nauvoo Legion in 1841 and warden of the music department of the University of Nauvoo the following year. He also served a mission to New England in 1842, then moved his family to Nauvoo a year after the martyrdom.

   The Billings moved west with the Saints in 1848, settling in the Sessions Settlement, later known as Bountiful. Titus was appointed to the Salt Lake Stake high council in 1849, then moved to Manti, Utah, that same year, where he was later called to serve as a counselor in the Sanpete stake presidency in 1851. Their family moved to the Provo, Utah, area most likely in 1864, where Titus passed away.

15. Lyman Wight and his wife, Harriet, played pivotal roles in the Restoration. Lyman was born in New York in 1796 and served in the War of 1812. He married Harriet Benton in 1823 and moved to Warrensville, Ohio, probably in 1826. He was baptized into the Reformed Baptist movement by Sidney Rigdon in May 1829, then moved to the Morley farm in February 1830. He and Harriet had moved to Mayfield shortly before being baptized into The Church of Jesus Christ of Latter-day Saints in November 1830. He was ordained an elder by Oliver Cowdery six days later, and in June 1831 he was ordained a high priest by Joseph Smith and ordained Joseph and Sidney Rigdon the same day.

Lyman was among the missionaries called to go to Missouri in Doctrine and Covenants 52 and traveled by way of Detroit and Pontiac, Michigan Territory. He was joined by his family in September 1831, then left them to serve a mission to Missouri, Ohio, and Virginia in January 1832. The Wights moved to the Big Blue settlement in Jackson County, where he presided over the branch there, then in November they were driven from Jackson into Clay County, Missouri. He recruited volunteers for and joined in Zion's Camp to Missouri in 1834. He was called as a member of the Clay County high council in 1834 where he served until moving to Caldwell County, Missouri, in 1837. He was elected colonel of the Caldwell County militia that same year, then moved his family to the area that became known as Adam-ondi-Ahman, Daviess County, Missouri, a year later.

Lyman served as a member of the Adam-ondi-Ahman stake presidency and was active in the "Mormon War." He was imprisoned with the Prophet and approximately sixty other brethren at Richmond, Ray County, Missouri, in November 1838. He was with Joseph in Liberty Jail beginning in November and allowed to escape to Quincy, Illinois, in April 1839. He was called to serve as a counselor to John Smith, president of the Lee County, Iowa, Branch that same year, then moved to Augusta, Des Moines County, Iowa, a year later. He was ordained a member of Quorum of the Twelve in April 1841 and served three missions that year and the two following.

Lyman served as a member of the Nauvoo City Council from 1841 to 1843. He led the brethren who obtained lumber for the Nauvoo Temple in Wisconsin in 1843 and 1844 and was appointed to the Council of Fifty. Following the martyrdom, he was rejected from the Council of Fifty in 1844, then led about 150 Latter-day Saints from the Wisconsin Territory to the Republic of Texas, arriving in November 1845. Unfortunately, he was excommunicated in 1848. Lyman died in Texas while en route to Jackson County, Missouri.

16. There are no known copies of Lyman Wight's journals, but portions were quoted in Joseph Smith III and Heman Smith, *The History of the Reorganized Church of Jesus Christ of Latter-day Saints* (Independence, MO: Herald House, 1896), 1:154.

17. Lucy Diantha Morley Allen, "Autobiographical Sketch," n.p., Morley Family Histories, MS 6106, Holograph, Church History Library, Salt Lake City.

18. Mary Lightner, "Mary Elizabeth Rollins Lightner," *Utah Genealogical and Historical Magazine* 17 (1926): 193–205; accessible online at http://boap.org/LDS/Early-Saints/MLightner.html.

19. Lightner, "Mary Elizabeth Rollins Lightner."

20. Lightner, "Mary Elizabeth Rollins Lightner."

21. Mary Lightner, "Mary Elizabeth Rollins Lightner."

22. "Fanaticism. The Golden Bible, or the Book of Mormon*,*" *The Geauga Gazette* (Painesville, OH), Feb. 1, 1831, 3.

23. Mary Elizabeth Lightner, Address at Brigham Young University, Apr. 14, 1905, typescript, Brigham Young University Archives and Manuscripts, https://contentdm.lib.byu.edu/digital/collection/p15999coll31/id/18292/.

24. Lightner, Address at Brigham Young University.

25. Lightner, Address at Brigham Young University.

26. Smith and Smith, *History of the Reorganized Church,* 1:316.

27. Esplin, "History of Isaac Morley."

28. History, 1838–1856, volume A-1 [23 December 1805–30 August 1834], 92–93, josephsmithpapers.org.

29. Larry C. Porter, "The Restoration of the Aaronic and Melchizedek Priesthoods," *Ensign*, Dec. 1996, 30–47.

30. Interview with James H. Hart, Mar. 18, 1884, as found in Ronald E. Romig, *Eighth Witness: The Biography of John Whitmer* (Independence, MO: John Whitmer Books, 2014), 25.

31. History, 1838–1856, volume A-1 [23 December 1805–30 August 1834], 26–27, josephsmithpapers.org.

32. "Historical Introduction," Revelation, circa August 1830 [D&C 27], josephsmithpapers.org.

33. *History of the Church,* 1:146.

34. John Whitmer, History, 1831–circa 1847, 11, josephsmithpapers.org.

35. Levi Hancock was born in Massachusetts two and a half years before the Prophet. He was among the original Kirtland converts baptized during the Lamanite mission. He married Clarissa Reed in March 1831, then was among the Missouri missionaries called to serve that same summer with Zebedee Coltrin. He participated in the organizational meeting of the School of the Prophets in January 1833 in the Whitney store and then in Zion's Camp in 1834. As a result, he was ordained a Seventy in 1835 and called as a president of the Seventy that same year. He moved his family with the body of the Saints to Caldwell County, Missouri, in 1838 and served as a member of a committee to assist the Saints in their removal from Missouri in early 1839. His family helped settle Nauvoo that year, and then as his family traveled with the early

company to the Rocky Mountains, he enlisted in the Mormon Battalion, the only General Authority to do so. He arrived in the Salt Lake Valley in 1847, was elected a member of the Utah territorial legislature for three terms in 1851, was ordained a patriarch in 1872, and died in Washington County, Utah, at the age of 79.

36. Heman Bassett was born in Vermont, moved to Ohio when he was about ten, lived on the Morley farm as part of the "family," and was baptized by January 1831 by the age of sixteen. He served a mission in northern Ohio that same year. He was called to be one of the Missouri missionaries in June 1831 but apparently denounced the Church, at least temporarily, and his call was revoked. He appears to have stayed with the Church, however, because he moved to Gallatin Township, Clay County, Missouri, by 1835, moved to Quincy, Illinois, by 1840 and to Keokuk, Iowa, across the Mississippi River from Nauvoo, by 1848. After the martyrdom, he joined the Strangites in New York City in 1849, was ordained an elder in that organization that same year, then moved to their headquarters near Racine, Wisconsin, in 1850. The Strangites excommunicated him in 1850, and he eventually found his way to Utah, then Sacramento, California, then Philadelphia, Pennsylvania, where he died in 1876.

37. Levi Hancock, "The life of Levi Hancock: Copies from his own journal by Clara E. H. Lloyd, great grand daughter," 28, St. George Utah FamilySearch Library, accessible online at https://www.familysearch.org/library/books/records/item/421997-the-life-of-levi-hancock-copies-from-his-own-journal-by-clara-e-h-lloyd-great-grand-daughter.

38. "Historical Introduction," Revelation, 4 February 1831 [D&C 41], josephsmithpapers.org.

39. *History of the Church*, 1:146–147.

40. The term "law" has a dual meaning in this and related verses—a general set of commandments and directions that lay a revealed foundation for the building of the kingdom, and the specific components that characterize the law of consecration.

41. John Whitmer's headnote to the copy of this revelation indicates that the issue leading to it was Leman Copley's invitation for Joseph and Sidney to bring their families and live on his farm (see verses 7–8). Joseph and his family were in need of housing because residing with the Whitneys was only a temporary situation, and Sidney and Phebe Rigdon needed housing because when they were converted, they had lost a house that was being constructed for them by Sidney's Campbellite congregation in Mentor. After the Rigdons were baptized, other Kirtland area converts invited their family moved in with them. Rigdon, "Lecture on the Early History of the Mormon Church," 14, 19–20, Church History Library, Salt Lake City.

42. Edward Partridge was a prosperous hatter in Painesville, Ohio, near Kirtland, and provided well for his wife, Lydia, and their children. He had religious leanings toward Universalism and Unitarianism but eventually joined with his wife as a follower of Sidney Rigdon and Alexander Campbell. Lydia was baptized when she heard the message of the Restoration taught by the Lamanite missionaries. Edward was not impressed with it, but he did send an employee to acquire a Book of Mormon for him. The book softened his heart toward their message, but he resisted baptism. He traveled to New York with Sidney Rigdon in December 1830 to meet the Prophet, which led to him being baptized.

Edward returned to Ohio and was called to the first bishop of the Church, "and this because his heart is pure before me, for he is like unto Nathanael of old, in whom there is no guile" (Doctrine and Covenants 41:11). Regarding his feelings about his service, he wrote to his wife, "You know I stand in an important station, and as I am occasionally chastened. I sometimes feel my station is above what I can perform to the acceptance of my Heavenly Father." Edward Partridge Jr., *Biography and Family Genealogy*, 6–7, Church History Library, Salt Lake City.

Edward was responsible for the implementation of the law of consecration, first in Kirtland and then in Missouri, thus helping provide for the Saints moving to both places through land acquisition and resource redistribution. From this point on, he and his family never enjoyed the level of financial security and comfort they had enjoyed prior to conversion. When mobocracy threatened the Missouri Saints in July 1833, Edward's attempts to mediate the situation led to him being forcefully removed from his home and physically abused. "I was taken from my house by the mob . . . who escorted me about half a mile, to the courthouse, on the public square in Independence; and then and there . . . I was stripped of my hat, coat and vest and daubed with tar from head to foot, and then had a quantity of feathers put upon me, and all this because I would not agree to leave the county, and my home where I had lived two years. . . . I bore my abuse with so much resignation and meekness, that it appeared to astound the multitude, who permitted me to retire in silence, many looking very solemn, their sympathies having been touched. And as to myself, I was so filled with the Spirit and love of God, that I had no hatred towards my persecutors or anyone else." History, 1838–1856, volume A-1 [23 December 1805–30 August 1834], 327, josephsmithpapers.org. He and his family escaped to Clay County in November with the Saints after camping on the Missouri River bank for five days and providing what comfort he could.

Edward and his family moved to Far West, Missouri, which only served as a temporary respite from persecution. The militia stole his hay and corn and tore down his animal shelter. He was among the approximately sixty brethren imprisoned in Far West and Richmond for a month. After fleeing with his family to Quincy, Illinois, he received lengthy instructions and encouragement for the Saints in a letter from which sections 121–123 were drawn. In Illinois he continued to live in poverty and experienced failing health. "I have not at this time two dollars in this world, one dollar and forty-four cents is all. I owe for my rent, and for making clothes for some of the poor, and some other things. . . . What is best for me to do, I hardly know. Hard labor I cannot perform; light labor I can; but I know of no chance to earn anything, at anything that I can stand to do. It is quite sickly here." Journal History of The Church of Jesus Christ of Latter-day Saints, June 13, 1839, Church History Library, Salt Lake City.

By the Nauvoo period, the Lord had established a system of multiple bishops serving the needs of geographic wards, and Edward was assigned to the Upper Ward. His service was short-lived. While attempting to build a home for his family in May 1840, he collapsed from exhaustion and passed away shortly thereafter. He was only forty-six years old. In recognition of his faithfulness, the Lord revealed to the Prophet Joseph Smith that He had received Edward Partridge "unto myself" (Doctrine and Covenants 124:19).

43. Section 42 also lists the "high council of the church," but this wording was added for the 1835 first edition of the Doctrine and Covenants. There was no high council until 1834 when the Kirtland Stake high council was formed, with the Prophet as president of the council and therefore the first stake president in Church history.

44. John Corrill first heard missionaries in Harpersville, Ohio, twenty-eight miles northeast of Kirtland, in January 1831. He wrote, "I was obliged to acknowledge in my own mind, that the meeting had been inspired by some supernatural agency." John Corrill, *A Brief History of the Church of Christ of Latter Day Saints*, 1839, 9, josephsmithpapers.org. After spending an evening with them, he was baptized in Kirtland, ordained an elder, then served a mission to New London, Ohio, where he first gained a reputation for being an effective missionary. He was ordained a high priest by Lyman Wight at the June 1831 conference on the Morley farm and called to serve with Lyman to Jackson County. He was joined by his family, and he served as second counselor to Bishop Edward Partridge. In July 1833, he, along with five other brethren including Edward, offered himself "as a ransom for the Church, expressing . . . willing[ness] to be scourged or to die if that would appease the anger of the mob against the Saints." History, 1838–1856, volume A-1 [23 December 1805–30 August 1834], 351, josephsmithpapers.org. He and his family were among those forced to flee their homes in November 1833 and escape to Clay County.

John surveyed Far West in conjunction with the Missouri legislature's designation of Caldwell County as a "reservation" for the Saints. A year later he was appointed "Keeper of the Lord's Store House" and subsequently elected a state legislator. With Elias Higbee, he was appointed a Church Historian in 1838. As persecution against the Saints increased, John "felt it was necessary for [him] to look out for [his] own safety" and distanced himself from the Church and subsequently testified against Joseph Smith and other Latter-day Saint prisoners when they were imprisoned in Richmond. John Corrill, *A Brief History of the Church of Christ of Latter Day Saints*, 1839, 37, josephsmithpapers.org. He stayed behind when the Saints fled Missouri in 1839 and was excommunicated that year by a disciplinary council in Quincy, Illinois. He also wrote *A Brief History of the Church of Latter-day Saints (commonly called Mormons), Including an Account of Their Doctrine and Discipline, with the Reasons of the Author for Leaving the Church*. He died near Quincy in 1841.

45. Revelation, 9 February 1831 [D&C 42:1–72], 6, josephsmithpapers.org.

46. John Whitmer, History, 1831–circa 1847, 23, josephsmithpapers.org.

47. John Whitmer, History, 1831–circa 1847, 23, josephsmithpapers.org.

48. "Historical Introduction," Revelation, 15 May 1831, josephsmithpapers.org.

49. Revelation, 15 May 1831, 85, josephsmithpapers.org.

50. Minute Book 2, 8, josephsmithpapers.org.

51. Lucy Mack Smith, History, 1844–1845, book 12, page 6, josephsmithpapers. org.

52. Revelation, 15 May 1831, 85, josephsmithpapers.org.

53. "Historical Introduction," Revelation, 20 May 1831 [D&C 51], josephsmithpapers.org.

54. Gerrit Dirkmaat, "10 Things You Didn't Know About Church History," *LDS Living*, Nov. 14, 2013, https://www.ldsliving. com/10-things-you-didnt-know-about-church-history/s/73991.

55. *History of the Church*, 1:364.

56. Leonard J. Arrington, Feramorz Y. Fox, and Dean L. May, *Building the City of God: Community & Cooperation Among the Mormons* (Salt Lake City, UT: Deseret Book, 1976), 28.

57. Levi Jackman, Deed of Consecration, MS 3103, Church History Library, Salt Lake City.

58. *History of the Church*, 1:341.

59. Joseph Knight Sr., Reminiscences, 9, MS 3470, Church History Library, Salt Lake City.

60. Joseph Knight Jr., Autobiographical Sketch (1862), MS 286, Church History Library, Salt Lake City.

61. John Whitmer, History, 1831–circa 1847, 29, josephsmithpapers.org.

62. Newel Knight, History, 307, MS 19156, Church History Library, Salt Lake City.

63. Parley P. Pratt, *The Autobiography of Parley Parker Pratt, One of the Twelve Apostles of the Church of Jesus Christ of Latter-day Saints: Embracing His Life, Ministry and Travels, With Extracts, in Prose and Verse, From His Miscellaneous Writings,* ed. Parley P. Pratt (Chicago, IL: Law, King & Law, 1888), 50.

64. Martin Luther, *Weimar Ausgabe*, 6:407, lines 19–25, cited in Timothy Wengert, "The Priesthood of All Believers and Other Pious Myths," *Institute of Liturgical Studies Occasional Papers* 2 (2005), https://scholar.valpo.edu/ils_papers/2/.

65. There is some question as to the actual name of Mrs. Hubble, or Hubbell. There was a Laura Fuller Hubbell who was the older sister of an early convert, Edson Fuller. However, Amos Hayden, in his book *Early Disciples of the Western Reserve*, lists a Mrs. Louisa Hubbell who was a member of the Disciples of Christ, temporarily accepted the restored gospel, and then rejoined the Disciples shortly thereafter. For our purposes, we will assume it's Laura Fuller Hubbell.

66. History, 1838–1856, volume A-1 [23 December 1805–30 August 1834], 101, josephsmithpapers.org.

67. History, 1838–1856, volume A-1 [23 December 1805–30 August 1834], 101, josephsmithpapers.org.

68. Ezra Booth, "Letter VIII," in Howe, *Mormonism Unvailed*, 216.

69. John Whitmer, History, 1831–circa 1847, 18, josephsmithpapers.org.

70. History, 1838–1856, volume A-1 [23 December 1805–30 August 1834], 101, josephsmithpapers.org.

71. John Whitmer, History, 1831–circa 1847, 18, josephsmithpapers.org.

72. Booth, "Letter VIII," 216.

73. [Matthew S. Clapp], "Mormonism," *Painesville Telegraph*, Feb. 15, 1831, [1]–[2].

74. John Whitmer, History, 1831–circa 1847, 10, josephsmithpapers.org.

75. John Whitmer, History, 1831–circa 1847, 26–27, josephsmithpapers.org.

76. Letter to Hyrum Smith, 3–4 March 1831, 1, josephsmithpapers.org.

77. John Corrill, *A Brief History of the Church of Christ of Latter Day Saints*, 1839, 24, josephsmithpapers.org.

78. *Autobiography of Parley Parker Pratt*, 61–62.

79. John Corrill, *A Brief History of the Church of Christ of Latter Day Saints*, 1839, 24, josephsmithpapers.org.

80. "Elder," Glossary, The Joseph Smith Papers, accessed Apr. 11, 2024, https://www.josephsmithpapers.org/topic/elder.

81. Jared Carter, Journal, 1831–1833, MS 1441, Church History Library, Salt Lake City.

82. Dean C. Jessee, "Joseph Knight's Recollection of Early Mormon History," *BYU Studies* 17, no. 1 (1976): 35.

83. John Whitmer, History, 1831–circa 1847, 24, josephsmithpapers.org.

84. "Historical Introduction," Revelation, circa 8 March 1831–B [D&C 47], josephsmithpapers.org.

85. Howe, *Mormonism Unvailed*, 216.

86. Edward W. Tullidge, ed., *Women of Mormondom* (New York: Tullidge & Crandall, 1877), 403.

87. Howe, *Moronism Unvailed*, 176.

88. Luke Johnson, "History of Luke Johnson," *Millennial Star,* Dec. 31, 1864, 834.

89. Philo Dibble, "Philo Dibble's Narrative," in *Early Scenes in Church History* (Salt Lake City, UT: Juvenile Instructor Office, 1882), 79.

90. Anderson, "The Western Reserve," in *Mapping Mormonism*, 28–29.

91. Church History Topics, "Church Discipline," Gospel Library.

92. Henry Carroll, "Statement," in *Naked Truths about Mormonism*, ed. Arthur Deming (Oakland, CA: Deming & Co., 1888), 2:3, 7.

93. George Albert Smith, in *Journal of Discourses*, 11:2.

94. John Whitmer, History, 1831–circa 1847, josephsmithpapers.org.

95. Minutes, 21 October 1831, 9, josephsmithpapers.org.

96. "John Whitmer copied the text into Revelation Book 1, where it is designated 'A prophecy March 7th. 1831.' Edward Partridge and William E. McLellin also made copies in 1831, but they assigned the date of 6 March 1831. The 1833 Book of Commandments dates this revelation to March 1831 and locates it at Kirtland, Ohio, while the 1835 Doctrine and Covenants specifies the date as 7 March but gives no location." "Historical Introduction," Revelation, circa 7 March 1831 [D&C 45], footnote 1, josephsmithpapers.org.

97. Revelation, circa 7 March 1831 [D&C 45], 71, josephsmithpapers.org. Note that the exact date of Joseph and Emma's move to the Morley farm is not known. It is fairly certain they were there by March 12 because that is the date when Martin Harris and his New York Branch arrived in Kirtland. Mary Elizabeth Rollins Lightner described a meeting the Prophet held with that group on the Morley farm when they arrived.

98. History, 1838–1856, volume A-1 [23 December 1805–30 August 1834], 104, josephsmithpapers.org.

99. *Autobiography of Parley P Pratt*, 48

100. Mark Lyman Staker, *Hearken, O Ye People: The Historical Setting of Joseph Smith's Ohio Revelations* (Salt Lake City, UT: Greg Kofford Books, 2009), 71.

101. Staker, *Hearken, O Ye People*, 73.

102. Staker, *Hearken, O Ye People*, 72.

103. Journal, 1832–1834, 84, josephsmithpapers.org.

104. Milton V. Backman, *The Heavens Resound: A History of the Latter-Day Saints in Ohio 1830–1838* (Salt Lake City, Utah: Deseret Book, 1983), 53.

105. Backman, *The Heavens Resound*, 53–54.

106. Backman, *The Heavens Resound*, 54.

107. History, 1838–1856, volume A-1 [23 December 1805–30 August 1834], 104, josephsmithpapers.org.

108. History, 1838–1856, volume A-1 [23 December 1805–30 August 1834], 104, josephsmithpapers.org.

109. Staker, *Hearken, O Ye People*, 45.

110. John W. Welch, "Oliver Cowdery's 1835 Response to Alexander Campbell's 1831 'Delusions,'" in Robert F. West, *Alexander Campbell and Natural Religion* (New Haven, CT: Yale University Press, 1948), 165.

111. Alexander Campbell, "Delusions," *Millennial Harbinger*, Feb. 7, 1831, 85–96; Alexander Campbell, *Delusions. An Analysis of the Book of Mormon; with an Examination of Its Internal and External Evidences, and a Refutation of Its Pretences to Divine Authority* (Boston: Benjamin H. Greene, 1832), 5–6. Accessible online at https://www.josephsmithpapers.org/intro/ introduction-to-documents-volume-2-july-1831-january-1833.

112. History, 1838–1856, volume A-1 [23 December 1805–30 August 1834], 104, josephsmithpapers.org.

113. Old Testament Revision 1, 1, josephsmithpapers.org.

114. "Source Note," Old Testament Revision 1, josephsmithpapers.org.

115. Revelation, 9 February 1831 [D&C 42:1–72], 1, josephsmithpapers.org.

116. History, 1838–1856, volume A-1 [23 December 1805–30 August 1834], 104, josephsmithpapers.org.

117. William W. Phelps, "Extract of a Letter from the Late Editor," *Ontario Phoenix* (Canandaigua, NY), Sept. 7, 1831, 2; History, 1838–1856, volume A-1 [23 December 1805–30 August 1834], 126, josephsmithpapers.org.

118. History, 1838–1856, volume A-1 [23 December 1805–30 August 1834], 127, josephsmithpapers.org.

119. Old Testament Revision 1, 1, josephsmithpapers.org.

120. New Testament Revision 1, 1, josephsmithpapers.org.

121. John Whitmer, History, 1831–circa 1847, 1, josephsmithpapers.org.

122. "Historical Introduction," John Whitmer, History, 1831–circa 1847, josephsmithpapers.org.

123. John Whitmer, History, 1831–circa 1847, 1, josephsmithpapers.org.

124. John Whitmer, History, 1831–circa 1847, 25, josephsmithpapers.org.

125. "Historical Introduction," John Whitmer, History, 1831–circa 1847, josephsmithpapers.org.

126. Articles and Covenants, circa April 1830 [D&C 20], 4, josephsmithpapers. org. Note that these verses reflect the verses' original composition prior to the editing associated with their publication.

127. Staker, *Hearken, All Ye People.*

128. Ezra Booth, "Mormonism—No. IV," *Ohio Star* (Ravenna, OH), Nov. 3, 1831, 3.

129. John Whitmer, History, 1831–circa 1847, 27, josephsmithpapers.org.

130. John Whitmer, History, 1831–circa 1847, 28–29, josephsmithpapers.org; History, 1838–1856, volume A-1 [23 December 1805–30 August 1834], 118, josephsmithpapers.org; see also 2 Thessalonians 2:3.

131. Booth, "Mormonism—No. IV," 3.

132. Jared Carter, Journal.

133. *Autobiography of Parley Parker Pratt*, 72.

134. Levi Hancock, Autobiography, ca. 1854, MS 8174, Church History Library, Salt Lake City.

135. John Whitmer, History, 1831–circa 1847, 27–28, josephsmithpapers.org.

136. The Joseph Smith Papers describes *commandment* as "generally, a divine mandate that church members were expected to obey; more specifically, a text dictated by JS in the first-person voice of Deity that served to communicate knowledge and instruction to JS and his followers." "Commandment," Glossary, The Joseph Smith Papers, accessed Apr. 11, 2024, https://www. josephsmithpapers.org/topic/commandment.

137. Minutes, circa 3–4 June 1831, josephsmithpapers.org.

138. *Autobiography of Parley Parker Pratt*, 72.

139. Levi Hancock, Autobiography.

140. John Whitmer, History, 1831–circa 1847, 27–28, josephsmithpapers.org.

141. Lyman Wight, Mountain Valley, TX, to Wilford Woodruff, [Salt Lake City, Utah Territory], 24 Aug. 1857, 5–6, Historian's Office, Histories of the Twelve, ca. 1858–1880, Church History Library, Salt Lake City.

142. Booth, "Mormonism—No. IV."

143. Levi Hancock, Autobiography.

144. Levi Hancock, Autobiography.

145. Levi Hancock, Autobiography.

146. Booth, "Mormonism—No. IV."

147. Levi Hancock, Autobiography.

148. Jared Carter, Journal.

149. Levi Hancock, Autobiography.

150. Levi Hancock, Autobiography.

151. *History of the Church*, 1:207.

152. *Teachings of Presidents of the Church: Joseph Smith* (2011), 186.

153. "Historical Introduction," Covenant of Oliver Cowdery and Others, 17 October 1830, josephsmithpapers.org.

154. Parley P. Pratt had traveled to St. Louis earlier to try to obtain permits to preach to the Lamanites but, when not successful, returned to Kirtland where he was called to go back to Missouri in company with his brother (see Doctrine and Covenants 52:26).

155. *Messenger and Advocate*, Sept. 1835, 179.

156. *Scraps of Biography: The Faith-Promoting Series Book 10* (Salt Lake City, UT: Juvenile Instructor Office, 1883), 70.

157. *Autobiography of Parley Parker Pratt*, 73.

158. Levi Hancock Diary, as found in Dennis Clegg, "Levi Ward Hancock: Pioneer, Soldier, Political and Religious Leader" (master's thesis, BYU, 1966), 55.

159. "The Life of Levi Hancock," unpublished manuscript, 54–64, L. Tom Perry Special Collections, Harold B. Lee Library, Brigham Young University, Provo.

160. "The Life of Levi Hancock."

161. History, 1838–1856, volume A-1 [23 December 1805–30 August 1834], 127, josephsmithpapers.org.

162. H. Michael Marquardt, "Ezra Booth on Early Mormonism: A Look at His 1831 Letters," *The John Whitmer Historical Association Journal* 28 (2008): 65–87.

163. Joseph Smith, "To the Elders of the Church of Latter Day Saints," *Messenger and Advocate*, Sept. 1835, 1:179.

164. There is some evidence that this information was foreshadowed by a previous unpublished revelation. "Calendar of Documents: 17 July 1831," The Joseph Smith Papers, accessed Apr. 11, 2024, https://www.josephsmithpapers.org/reference/calendar-of-documents#1831-07.

165. "Jew" here refers to the Lamanites, and "Gentile" to the white settlers (i.e., the line refers to the western border of Missouri that bordered unincorporated "Indian lands"). "Historical Introduction," Revelation, 20 July 1831 [D&C 57], footnote 7, josephsmithpapers.org.

166. "Historical Introduction," Revelation, 1 August 1831 [D&C 58], josephsmithpapers.org.

167. Letter, Aug. 5, 1831, in Edward Partridge letters, 1831–1835, Church History Library, Salt Lake City.

168. History, 1838–1856, volume A-1 [23 December 1805–30 August 1834], 137, josephsmithpapers.org.

169. *History of the Church*, 1:196.

170. F. Mark McKiernan and Roger D. Launius, eds., *An Early Latter Day Saint History: The Book of John Whitmer* (Independence, MO: Herald Publishing House, 1980), 7.

171. Description by Oliver Cowdery copied into *The Book of John Whitmer Kept by Commandment*, chapter 9, circa 1836, Community of Christ Library-Archives, Independence, Missouri.

172. *History of the Church*, 1:199.

173. "Historical Introduction," Minutes, 4 August 1831, josephsmithpapers.org.

174. Minutes, 4 August 1831, 5, josephsmithpapers.org.

175. *Scraps of Biography*, 70.

176. William W. Phelps, "Extract of a Letter from the Late Editor," *Ontario Phoenix* (Canandaigua, NY), Sept. 7, 1831.

177. "Church History," 1 March 1842, 708, josephsmithpapers.org.

178. T. Edgar Lyon, "Independence, Missouri, and the Mormons, 1827–1833," *BYU Studies* 13, no. 1 (1972): 16.

179. William G. Hartley, *My Fellow Servants: Essays on the History of the Priesthood* (Provo, UT: BYU Studies, 2010), 343–344.

180. Ezra Booth, "Mormonism—No. VI," *Ohio Star* (Ravenna, OH), Nov. 17, 1831, 3.

181. Booth, "Mormonism—No. VI," 3.

182. History, 1838–1856, volume A-1 [23 December 1805–30 August 1834], 141, josephsmithpapers.org.

183. Ezra Booth, "Mormonism—No. V," *Ohio Star* (Ravenna, OH), Nov. 10, 1831, 3.

184. *History of the Church*, 1:202–3.

185. From John Whitmer's original heading for the revelation. "Historical Introduction," Revelation, 12 August 1831 [D&C 61], josephsmithpapers.org.

186. Wetmore, *Gazetteer of the State of Missouri*, 33–35, cited in "Historical Introduction," Revelation, 12 August 1831 [D&C 61], josephsmithpapers.org.

187. Howe, *Mormonism Unvailed*, 204.

188. Ezra Booth to Edward Partridge, Sept. 20, 1831, in the *Ohio Star*, Nov. 24, 1831.

189. *History of the Church*, 1:202–3.

190. Journal History of The Church of Jesus Christ of Latter-day Saints, Aug. 13, 1831, Church History Library, Salt Lake City.

191. History, 1838–1856, volume A-1 [23 December 1805–30 August 1834], 145, josephsmithpapers.org.

192. The Joseph Smith Papers provides an interesting description of the Missouri Saints' reaction to reading the revelation contained in section 62 when it was brought to them. "According to Hancock's account, when the Saints in Jackson County saw a copy of this revelation—probably brought to them by one of the four elders to whom it was directed—it 'tried' their faith. The revelation's contents, which included commendations of those who had borne testimony and which implied high expectations for proselytizing success, apparently struck the Missouri Saints as incongruous with the results of the elders' preaching. As Elizabeth Van Benthusen Gilbert explained to Hancock, 'Their faith almost failed them because they had heard that nothing was done.' In reference to the elders, she said that 'many had appostatized.' After Hancock, Zebedee Coltrin, Simeon Carter, and Solomon Hancock arrived later in the fall with news that they had baptized over a hundred individuals, the 'drooping Spirits' of the Missouri Saints were 'revived.'" "Autobiography of Levi Ward Hancock," ca. 1896, 40–41, cited in "Historical Introduction," Revelation, 13 August 1831 [D&C 62], footnote 8, josephsmithpapers.org.

193. John Whitmer, History, 1831–circa 1847, 33, josephsmithpapers.org.

194. John Whitmer, History, 1831–circa 1847, 133, josephsmithpapers.org.

195. "William McLellin to Relatives, 4 Aug 1832, typescript, RLDS Archives," Book of Abraham Project, accessed Apr. 11, 2024, http://boap.org/LDS/Early-Saints/Mcllelin.html.

196. History, 1838–1856, volume A-1 [23 December 1805–30 August 1834], 146, josephsmithpapers.org.

197. John Whitmer, History, 1831–circa 1847, 33, josephsmithpapers.org.

198. History, 1838–1856, volume A-1 [23 December 1805–30 August 1834], 146, josephsmithpapers.org.

199. Minute Book 2, 23, josephsmithpapers.org; Letter from Oliver Cowdery, 28 January 1832, josephsmithpapers.org.

200. Minute Book 2, 23, josephsmithpapers.org; Letter from Oliver Cowdery, 28 January 1832, josephsmithpapers.org.

201. For more information about Ezra Booth, see Damon Bahr and Thomas P. Aardema, *The Voice of the Lord is Unto All Men: A Remarkable Year of Revelations in the Johnson Home* (Springville, UT: Cedar Fort, 2021).

202. Lawrence R. Flake, "A Shaker View of a Mormon Mission," *BYU Studies* 20, no. 1 (Fall 1979): 95.

203. Flake, "A Shaker View," 95.

204. Flake, "A Shaker View," 95.

205. Flake, "A Shaker View," 95–96.

206. History, 1838–1856, volume A-1 [23 December 1805–30 August 1834], 112, josephsmithpapers.org.

207. History, 1838–1856, volume A-1 [23 December 1805–30 August 1834], 112, josephsmithpapers.org.

208. John Whitmer, History, 1831–circa 1847, 26, josephsmithpapers.org.

209. Flake, "A Shaker View," 97.

210. Flake, "A Shaker View," 97.

211. Flake, "A Shaker View," 97–98.

212. Flake, "A Shaker View," 98.

213. Flake, "A Shaker View," 98.

214. Flake, "A Shaker View," 98–99.

215. David W. Grua, "Joseph Smith and the 1834 D. P. Hurlbut Case," *BYU Studies* 44, no. 1 (2005): 33–54.

216. History, 1838–1856, volume B-1 [1 September 1834–2 November 1838], 726, josephsmithpapers.org.

217. *Deseret News*, May 20, 1886, cited in Andrew Jenson, "Plural Marriage," *Historical Record* 6 (July 1887): 219.

218. Joseph B. Noble speaking at a quarterly stake conference held at Centerville, Davis County, Utah, June 11, 1883, cited in Jenson, "Plural Marriage," 232–33.

219. Staker, *Hearken, O Ye People*, 117 (footnote 2).

220. W. W. Phelps to Brigham Young, August 12, 1861, Young Collection, Church History Library, Salt Lake City, copy of holograph in possession of the Brian C Hales, cited in Brian C. Hales, "1830s," Joseph Smith's Polygamy, accessed Apr. 12, 2024, https://josephsmithspolygamy.org/history/polygamy-early-1830s/.

221. Joseph Smith, in Conference Report, Apr. 1898, 57.

222. *Church Almanac: 2013* (Salt Lake City, UT: Deseret Book, 2012).

223. Council of Fifty, Minutes, March 1844–January 1846; Volume 3, 6 May 1845–13 January 1846, 85, josephsmithpapers.org; "Rocky Mountains, North America," The Joseph Smith Papers, accessed Apr. 12, 2024, https://www.josephsmithpapers.org/place/rocky-mountains-north-america.

224. "Facts and Statistics," *Newsroom*, accessed Apr. 12, 2024, https://newsroom.churchofjesuschrist.org/facts-and-statistics.

Damon L. Bahr   Thomas P. Aardema

ABOUT THE AUTHORS

At the time this book was written, Damon L. Bahr was an associate professor in the Department of Teacher Education at Brigham Young University where he taught courses in mathematics education. He also taught in the BYU Department of Church History and Doctrine where he taught courses in the Doctrine and Covenants. Damon is a frequent presenter at BYU Education Week and enjoys conducting tours of Church history sites, especially in Kirtland. He served a mission to Australia as a young man, then he and his wife, Kim, served a mission at the Kirtland historic sites. They are the parents of four children and grandparents to eighteen.

Thomas P. Aardema is a Region Director of Seminaries and Institutes, with his office near the historic Johnson home in Hiram, Ohio. He has taught seminary and institute for over twenty years and has lived and taught in the Kirtland area for over ten years. He received a BA in history from Weber State University, an MBA from the University of Utah, and a PhD in education from Utah State University. He and his wife, Emilee, are the parents of five sons. He loves Church history and feels blessed to live, teach, and serve near the sacred sites of Church history.